AMERICA'S MOUNTAINS

**An Exploration of Their Origins and Influences
from the Alaska Range to the Appalachians**

Clark Hubler

Facts On File®

AN INFOBASE HOLDINGS COMPANY

**America's Mountains: An Exploration of Their Origins and
Influence from the Alaska Range to the Appalachians**

Facts On File, Inc.
460 Park Avenue South
New York NY 10016

Library of Congress Cataloging-in-Publication Data

Hubler, Clark.
    America's mountains : an exploration of their origins and
influences from the Alaska Range to the Appalachians / Clark Hubler.
      p.   cm.
    Includes bibliographical references and index.
    ISBN 0-8160-2661-0 (acid-free)
    1. Orogeny—North America.   I. Title.
QE621.5.N7H83   1995   94-15321
551.8'2'097—dc20

Facts On File books are available at special discounts when purchased in bulk quantities
for businesses, associations, institutions or sales promotions. Please call our Special Sales
Department in New York at 212/683-2244 or 800/322-8755.

Text and jacket design by Robert Yaffe

Printed in the United States of America

RRD FOF 10 9 8 7 6 5 4 3 2 1

This book is printed on acid-free paper

Table of Contents

Introduction   v

1 Mountain Building in the West Today   1

2 Mountains' Influence on Life   25

3 Uplift of the Rocky Mountains and the Southwest   37

4 Uplift of the Appalachians   53

5 Mountains and Glaciers   87

6 Plains and Plateaus   119

7 Rocks, Fossils, and Mountains   143

8 Mountains of the Past   167

9 Midocean Ridges and Terranes   173

Appendices

   Table 1:   Estimated Dates of Major Transitions
              in Geological History   183

   Table 2:   Geological Time Scale   184

   Table 3:   Estimates of Geological Time   185

   Table 4:   Some Common Rocks   186

   Table 5:   Relationships of Common Rocks   187

Index   189

Introduction

When our grandparents and great-grandparents were schoolchildren, geography books were still explaining that mountains were simply wrinkles on the surface of the Earth. The books said the Earth was cooling and shrinking like a baked apple—wrinkling as it cooled.

In ancient times, people had even stranger ideas of how mountains came to be the way they are. A learned Greek mathematician and philosopher, Pythagoras, explained that underground winds caused mountains and hills to bulge upward, much as blowing causes a balloon to expand. Pliny, a Roman historian, wrote that nature had made the mountains in order to strengthen the earth against swift streams and the huge waves which sometimes pound against the shores. Avicenna, an ancient Persian philosopher, had another idea. He explained that winds and floods carry away some of the land and leave other parts standing as highlands, which in some cases is true. However, he also told how some mountains are forced upward by winds caused by violent earthquakes. During the Middle Ages in Italy, Albertus Magnus, a competent student of minerals, stated that volcanoes are caused by underground fires that cause the surface to explode and raise mountains. Also in the Middle Ages, Ristoro, an Italian artisan, concluded from his study of the stars that they are like magnets, drawing away the water to form oceans and leaving the dry lands as hills and mountains.

Fearsome giants and mysterious spirits long ago occupied the mountaintops almost everywhere. In Norway, for example, evil giants were said to have lived in the mountains of Jotunheimen. According to a German myth, centuries ago the mountains and valleys of Germany were formed by giants stomping on soft ground that has since hardened. Lowlands were formed where the ground was pressed down under the weight of the giants, with highlands forced upward around their feet. In American folk tales, Paul Bunyan dug Puget Sound in western Washington with a huge shovel. As he was digging, he tossed the dirt aside, to his left and to his right, creating on one side the Cascade Range and on the other side the Olympic Mountains of Puget Sound.

Though the tall tales told about the creation of mountains are fascinating, the truth is even more so. Consider the volcanic lava and pumice of which some mountains are built. Likewise, the gigantic faults along which mountains have been shoved upward, or the rugged canyons and gorges cut into uplifted plateaus. Dinosaur bones can be seen in the mountainous ground of Utah and Colorado, and the reptiles' footprints in what is now the solid rock of the Connecticut Valley. Volcanoes and lava flows are sensational in the West. Likewise, it is fascinating to see where similar eruptions have occurred in the East from Maine to Alabama.

We may not believe, as related in Native American folklore, that Mount Mazama in Oregon got into a fight with Mount Shasta in California. The two of them were hurling fiery stones at each other. The fight ended when Mazama, the evil one, collapsed and fell back into a hole—the hole that is now Crater Lake. Yet more fantastic than anything imagined by the Indians is the idea that South America could have been where the Gulf of Mexico is today. Nevertheless, geologists find sediments on the coastal plain of Texas that may have washed off a landmass to the south—presumably South America.

Earthquakes that shake everything in sight are common in the West. They are the "growing pains" of mountain building. Such disturbances are no longer common in the East, yet evidence of great earthquakes can be found throughout the Appalachians, where mountains of the distant past were shoved inland along distinct fault lines. The mountains were shoved upward, and the disturbances caused severe tremors when rocks broke under pressure.

There is so much to be seen, including the "Craters of the Moon" at a national park of that name in Idaho, where there are lava flows just like those on the moon. The Ice Age is not over in Montana, where glaciers continue to move, carving jagged peaks and rounded valleys. In Glacier Park even a mountain has been moved along a great fault, shoved eastward more than 15 miles. Chief Mountain now stands alone on the edge of the Great Plains.

In Wyoming there is a solid rock spire named Devil's Tower. According to an Indian legend, seven little girls were playing near the rock. Threatened by a very large bear, the girls climbed onto the rock, and the big rock promptly rose high into the sky, well out of reach. The bear left claw marks on the sides of the rock while trying to get to the girls. Those girls are still up in the sky out of harm's way, forming a cluster of stars our European ancestors named the Pleiades. Geologists have a different opinion about the tower, reporting that it is a volcanic neck, the center of a former volcano with surrounding rocks worn away. In that view, the claw marks are actually columnar jointing, cracks formed as the molten rock of the volcano cooled and shrank.

Geologists today are coming up with some equally fantastic accounts to explain the tremendous phenomena they witness. In their view, North America, Africa, and other continents are drifting about on the surface of an Earth that is not entirely rigid. Moreover, the West Coast of California south of San Francisco is slowly drifting northward in relation to the main body of North America. West of the San Andreas Fault in California the land is moving about two inches a year, which is not much. But over thousands, even millions, of years that movement can make a difference. The broken rocks along the fault bind, then suddenly give way; the jolting tremors create an earthquake, sometimes severe, but more often not. Such disturbances are indicative of mountain building today.

Across America, there is always something impressive to see. Oklahoma is certainly a stable area; yet it revealed a fault line when a small stream was diverted by an uplift along one side of an old fault—an entirely harmless yet interesting example of how such changes shape our land. Anyone in Denver can gain a new appreciation of the imposing mountains west of the city simply by gaining an understanding of how those mountains came to be uplifted along a major fault line of broken rocks. Georgia's Granite Mountain is only a remnant of once-lofty mountains, while the beauty of the nearby Blue Ridge Parkway also tells a story of how the mountains came to be.

In celebrating the bicentennial of the American Constitution, a memorial was built at the nation's capital of rocks from all 50 states: granite from a historical quarry in Delaware, colorful limestone from New Mexico, a boulder of silver ore from Nevada, and other such representative stones. The monument built of these stones serves to honor what our constitution represents, but incidentally it also provides recognition of our human interest in the rocks that have shaped the land where we live.

Mountains are attractive to people for a variety of reasons, and that fascination is expressed in numerous ways. In the winter, New Englanders and others head for the ski slopes of the White Mountains in New Hampshire and the Green Mountains of Vermont. At Acadia National Park, Cadillac Mountain provides a broad view of the Atlantic. In addition to skiing, the mountains provide winter playgrounds for tobogganing, sledding, snowmobiling, and much more. Affluent families have summer homes on mountainsides in Maine where they can enjoy the scenery in cool splendor. Aerial chair lifts are available at many sites, providing wide views of the mountains for sightseeing. Campgrounds are plentiful in many locations.

In eastern Pennsylvania, the Pocono Mountains provide many recreational sites, as do the Allegheny Mountains farther west. Fishing, hunting, and winter sports are among the featured attractions.

Scenic drives attract many tourists to the Black Hills of South Dakota. Mount Rushmore is one of the interesting attractions. West of Lake Superior, in the mountainous areas of Minnesota, winter sports are featured. In the Mountain State, West Virginia, there are numerous views for sightseeing, as from the overlook at the summit of East River Mountain, a short way south of Bluefield, and from the Hawk's Nest overlooking the New River.

In the Ozark highlands of Arkansas, where there are numerous lakes, duck hunting in the fall season attracts many sportsmen. As we gain fascinating insights regarding the way mountains are uplifted and then change, the scenic views become even more engrossing.

In the Far West, a resort on the lower slopes of Mount Hood is much admired; Timberline Lodge is both luxurious and picturesque, as are the lodges at most mountain resorts. Tourists and many local people spend considerable time on the lower slopes of Mount Hood, a noted prominence in sight of Portland, Oregon. Mount Rainier likewise is a prominent resort area in full view from Seattle and Tacoma, enjoyed by residents and visitors to Washington's Puget Sound region. Across the sound, the Olympic Mountains feature cool and comfortable sightseeing.

Mountain climbing appeals to those who are energetic and adventuresome, but there are many less strenuous activities available to those who enjoy the mountains. Skiing is an attraction on the slopes of Mount Baker, out from Bellingham, Washington. The ski area is located on the slopes between Mount Baker and Mount Shucksan. The ice field and glacier at the top of Shucksan are a spectacular sight. More such glaciers can be seen on Mount Baker. For family fun, picking blueberries on the mountainsides below the snow line is a common outing.

Throughout America, the national parks of the United States and Canada feature spectacular mountain scenery and pleasant facilities for visitors. The scenery is not only impressive and awe inspiring but also serves as a change of pace for many visitors. The back-to-nature sights bring an environmental emphasis to the daily routines of our intricate modern lives.

Most of the prominent Canadian mountains are in the Far West, where scenery is abundant. On the border, contiguous with Glacier National Park in Montana, is the Canadian Watertown Lakes National Park. Among the glacial mountain peaks are hotel and cabin accommodations for tourists, plus well-equipped campgrounds. A bit farther north, national parks at Jasper and nearby Banff are among the noted mountain resorts of Canada. These and other popular Canadian resorts feature majestic mountain peaks, ice fields, natural hot springs, and winter sports.

The Trans-Canada Highway extends from Vancouver, British Columbia, through spectacular mountain scenery where highways lead off into ever more abundant scenic views of mountains and glaciers, to Jasper and Banff, thence across the broad Canadian Shield. There, only the stumps of once lofty mountains remain as jumbles of hard rocks that tell a fabulous story of the past. Good views of the flat surfaces of ancient rocks can be seen at many points along the highway. From north of Lake Superior, the Trans-Canada Highway continues beyond Montreal on the south side of the Saint Lawrence River. At Quebec the heights on the north bank of the river had a prominent place in history. English troops surmounted the cliffs to capture a vital French fort in a surprise attack during the French and Indian War. The Trans-Canada Highway continues to the Atlantic, through the formerly rugged Appalachian Mountains and on to the peninsula of Nova Scotia and Cape Breton Island.

Volcanic eruptions, earthquakes, and rugged mountains all serve to indicate that mountain building is occurring in the West today. When Mount Saint Helens erupted in 1980, geologists came from far and wide to see for themselves what was happening. We can all learn in much the same way. What is going on in the West today not only is interesting but also provides a continuing demonstration of how mountains are built. So in this book we begin with the same dynamic approach, for the realities of today are both stimulating and meaningful.

In the East, when we see evidence of what happened in the past, we can understand its similarity to what is happening in mountain building today, even in the older mountains where the changes have been profound, where the rocks of once lofty mountains have crumbled in the weather. Streams have washed the sediment into the lowlands, a process continuing even now, changing the old mountains and the lowlands as well. The rocks of the Appalachians now on the surface are but the stumps of tall mountains, for the rocks above have been worn away.

Continuing, we delve more deeply into the past, considering the Canadian Shield, where still older mountains once stood. In going from the present to the past, we can begin to understand even the extremely distant past.

By considering what mountain glaciers in the West are like, we gain some understanding of the Ice Age, when massive glaciers covered almost all of Canada and large areas in northern portions of the United States. The rocks and fossils imbedded in glaciers provide additional evidence of what has happened in the past.

Mountains have a marked influence on the weather, hence also on vegetation. Animals too are affected, and so are people. So life on Earth is deeply influenced by mountain building. Therefore geologists use periods of mountain building to mark the divisions of time in which conditions on Earth have changed, for the mountains influence everything on Earth. In normal affairs we record events in terms of years, but in the very distant past there were no people on Earth to keep a record of the years; so geological history is recorded in terms of the mountains. For example, whatever occurred before the Rocky Mountains were built, but since the Appalachians were uplifted, is known as the Mesozoic Era, which means middle life. Times in geological history sometimes are spoken of in terms of years, yet those numbers are but estimates. In the past such estimates have been inadequate, but better estimates have been found with newer methods.

Altogether this book seeks to reveal some of the fascination with our environment, without becoming excessively involved with the complexities of geology. Nevertheless it has become evident that with such an introduction to the realities of today, an appreciable number of individuals can become sufficiently enthused to delve further into the dynamics of earth science.

1

MOUNTAIN BUILDING IN THE WEST TODAY

Massive mountain ranges bordering the west coast of the United States extend northward through western Canada into Alaska. These mountains are also prominent throughout Central America and along the west coast of South America. How they came to be and how they continue to evolve constitutes a fascinating geological account.

5:00 P.M., October 17, 1989. A young woman in Santa Clara, California, at the southern end of San Francisco Bay, talks on the telephone to her sister at home, 20 miles farther south in the hill country inland from Santa Cruz. During the telephone conversation, the connection is abruptly lost. Seconds later the sister in Santa Clara feels the tremors of a violent earthquake. Finally the disturbance reaches San Francisco and Oakland on opposite sides of the bay.

That earthquake originated in the San Andreas Fault, which extends through the Santa Cruz Mountains. The disturbance, called the Loma Prieta Earthquake, after the tallest mountain in the vicinity, reached San Francisco and Oakland in 25 seconds. Near the epicenter in Santa Cruz, where the rocks of the San Andreas Fault jolted loose, damage was severe, but farther away in San Jose and Santa Clara the destruction was comparatively minor. Farther north in San Francisco and Oakland the devastation was great. Sections of an elevated highway in Oakland and a long bridge across the bay collapsed, and numerous buildings were destroyed, especially in the Marina District of San Francisco. Altogether, the quake took 67 lives, and property damage was estimated to have been in the billions of dollars.

Why the damage was greater farther north on both sides of the bay than at intermediate distances, such as at Santa Clara, is due to two major factors. Damage is known to be more severe where structures have been erected on filled land, rather than on firm ground or solid rock. The Marina District of San Francisco is an example of an area on filled land. Also, the tremors of an earthquake spread outward in all directions as do waves on water. In this case, the back-and-forth motion of the waves was reflected off the hard rocks at great depth in such a way as to be focused upward onto the vulnerable cities.

Earthquakes As Evidence of Mountain Building

In California the major source of earthquakes is the San Andreas Fault, where the rocks visible at the surface and extending to great depths are broken, yet in close contact. Geologists explain that the American continent is gradually drifting westward, keeping the broken rocks of the fault tightly pressed together. The rocks on the shoreward side of the fault are joined firmly to those of the ocean basin, which are likewise drifting, but in a different direction, northward. Along the fault where the broken rocks are pressed together, the northward movement is resisted until eventually the west side jolts loose and moves a short way north, the resulting tremors spreading out as the vibrations of an earthquake.

The San Andreas Fault extends diagonally southward through the eastern suburbs of Los Angeles, through the Salton Sea and Imperial Valley, and into the Gulf of California, where it separates Lower California from the mainland of Mexico. Los Angeles and San Diego, together with all the land west of the fault, including Lower California, are firmly attached to the ocean bed that is gradually drifting northward, but the movement is sufficient to cause serious earthquakes when it breaks loose at the fault line. Northward from Point Reyes (about 30 miles north of San Francisco), the fault line lies offshore and underwater, which may explain why the earthquakes are less severe in the Pacific Northwest. Nevertheless, the rugged mountains of the region provide definitive evidence of serious upheavals, with the threat of consequent earthquakes always hanging in the air.

Farther north in Alaska, where the Pacific plates of the ocean bottom encounter the Alaskan mainland and peninsula, earthquakes and mountain building are frequent and often severe, even by Alaskan standards. The earthquake on March 27, 1964, provides a notable example. It was late in the day in Anchorage. Some office building occupants sought comparative safety in doorways, closets, or narrow halls, but some fell as they attempted to cross the swaying floors. Wood and plaster could be heard ripping apart. Broad cracks opened in walls. Books tumbled from shelves, while typewriters and calculators clattered to the floor and office furniture slid about. The lights went out as lamp fixtures overhead jerked from side to side, accompanied by the grinding, rumbling sounds of destruction.

The episode lasted five minutes. Offices were a shambles. Bookcases had tumbled over, and large pictures dislodged from the walls lay broken on the floors. Likewise in stores, produce from the shelves had tumbled down. People rushed out onto the streets shouting. Blocks of concrete from the pavement were upended in the streets. Rubble continued to fall from the buildings. One whole section of the Anchorage Federal Savings building suddenly collapsed. Massive blocks fallen from buildings had crushed cars parked below. One whole side of the J. C. Penney building was hanging precariously, ready to come down. On Fourth Avenue, a camera shop, pawn shop, and adjoining stores had sunk below street level. One long building dipped into the cavity, slanting upward above the street like a ship riding waves at sea. The Alaska Sales and Service building had collapsed into rubble. Those who found their automobiles undamaged got in and attempted to drive out into the residential areas but found the streets broken, power lines down, and water gushing into the streets from broken mains and sewer pipes.

In the residential areas of Anchorage, large fissures had opened in yards and in the foundations of some houses. One whole section of view property on Turnagain Heights, containing the finest homes of the city, had been carried away on a landslide into the waters of Turnagain Inlet. Other homes were left hanging on the edge of the bluff, ready to slide farther at the next disturbance.

Anchorage, the largest city of Alaska, was hit especially hard, not only by the magnitude of the quake but also because of the soft sediments on which the city was built. Those sediments readily transmitted the violent oscillations, causing unequal settling, landslides, and damage to foundations. In contrast, the damage at Cordova was much less. Cordova, a small city east of Anchorage, is built on solid rock.

The Alaska Mountain Range

The Alaska Mountain Range, in sight north of Anchorage, extends southwest along the Alaska Peninsula, with the Aleutian Islands as a further extension of the mountain range pointing toward Japan. The inland Mount McKinley, the highest peak in North America at 20,320 feet, and the rugged peninsula and the Aleutian Islands provide a range of mountains that serve as an ideal example of mountain building now under way.

As the rocks of the ocean bed relentlessly drift northward, they press firmly against the land mass of Alaska. The dense black basalt rock of the ocean bed tends to dip beneath the lighter rocks of the land, compressing and lifting that land to form mountains. The pressure is persistent, but the uplift is not uniform. Granite and other rocks of the land bind and stand firm as the relentless pressure mounts, but eventually the rocks break and jolt free. The result is an earthquake with the land mass bulging upward. Under the pressure some areas are crumpled and bent downward, depressed.

The great Alaskan earthquake has provided some of the best evidence of how mountain ranges are uplifted. In many places the uplift was readily apparent. Docks, canneries, and other waterfront buildings were elevated so high above the water that they couldn't be reached by the boats of customers. Watermarks where waves had cut into seacliffs were no longer at water level but high above. Where the slope of the shore was more gradual, a wide expanse of sand and gravel beach separated the old shoreline from the water. Great areas of mud were left high and dry, forming a pattern of mud cracks on a dry surface. Barnacles and certain types of algae that normally live no higher than the water level were found far above on the sides of rocky cliffs. Barnacle heights above the water were measured in many places. As new barnacles began to grow at the lower water level, the differences in the two heights served as a check on other measurements. Sea level can be difficult to determine as tides come and go. Onshore winds tend to increase the water level. Though sea level can be established with accuracy over a period of time, immediate changes are more difficult to determine. Nevertheless, tide-gauge readings like those using the barnacles indicated a great change. Near the highways geologists and civil engineers had earlier established "bench marks," brass markers on solid rock or concrete posts recording the height of the land. New surveys revealed that changes had occurred.

Montague Island is located in the region of greatest uplift. A portion of the island was elevated about 33 feet. The ocean bottom nearby was found to have been uplifted as much as 49 feet. The average there seems to have been somewhat more than six feet. Another smaller area between Kodiak Island and Anchorage became depressed a little more than six feet below the old level.

The deformation of the ocean bottom formed a trough, uplifted on two sides and depressed between. The adjoining land was likewise uplifted somewhat. The Alaska Range, along with Mount McKinley, was probably further elevated about two feet, but the amount has not been confirmed. The great Alaskan earthquake, as destructive as it was, did provide geologists with a fine example of mountain building. Each earthquake marks a release of pressures and further uplift of the land. Over a period of time mountains are built near the coast, each disturbance lifting the land higher.

Geological records list about 90 severe earthquakes in the Anchorage area during the previous 180 years, an average of one every second year. In addition, there have been innumerable lesser disturbances, each adding to the elevation of the mountains. The great earthquake of 1964 has been assigned a magnitude of 8.4 on a logarithmic scale upward from zero. As such it is one of the most violent earthquakes known.

After the earthquake it was found that nearby Cordova, although not severely damaged, was about eight feet higher than before. To the west, bordering the Gulf of Alaska, the towns of Whittier, Seward, and Kodiak each sank about five feet, indicative of folding under pressure. In the same gulf area, after the subsidence, the entire business section of Seldovia and much of Homer's became flooded during each high tide. Farther south on the mainland, Valdez was elevated about 10 feet. The town has had to be relocated farther inland, for much of the previous location was destroyed in a waterfront landslide.

Near the earthquake center, where the Gulf of Alaska is bordered by the Kenai Peninsula and a chain of islands, the ocean bottom was uplifted during the disturbance. As a result the water itself was uplifted and began to flow outward in all directions, forming the initial wave of what often is called a great "tidal wave" but properly is designated a *tsunami*. At some points the waves were said to be 30 to 35 feet high. That tsunami wreaked havoc on coastal communities, many of them far away. The farther a wave spreads, the smaller it becomes, as can be seen by tossing a stone into a quiet pond. Yet the shape of the shoreline where the big wave strikes can influence the height of the waves and the damage done. Seward, on the Kenai Peninsula, for example, is located at the narrow end of an inlet that acted as a funnel. The waves that poured in at the open end became even higher as the inlet narrowed. Consequently the waterfront was demolished.

By the time the great waves had spread as far as the coast of California, they were no longer as high. Yet at Crescent City, north of San Francisco, the business district was damaged and 10 people drowned. The gradual slope of the shore at Crescent City in a sense tripped the wave at its base and projected it into the city with increased force. That boats, boxcars, and even a locomotive were tossed onto the shore testifies to the force of the tsunami waves at their height.

Other Sites of Mountain Building

In California the San Andreas Fault extends northward from Point Reyes off the coast. In the Pacific Northwest that main fault continues but at a considerable distance from shore. Smaller segments of the ocean bottom, close to shore, are being subducted, that is, depressed beneath the North American continent, producing eruptions such as that of Mount Saint Helens. Geologists now have become concerned that strains developing along the fault lines of these smaller plates could cause a serious disturbance under water. An abrupt break in the fault-line rocks could cause a section of ocean bed to be jolted upward, elevated several feet. The water there, as in Alaska, would be uplifted, and the result could be a major tsunami along the coast. Serious damage to shoreline communities of Vancouver Island, Washington, and Oregon could result. The devastation could be great at such cities as Astoria, at the mouth of the Columbia River, and also at Aberdeen and Hoquium on Grays Harbor. The threat is less for cities such as Seattle, Victoria, and Vancouver, for the high waves would have to traverse the Strait of Juan de Fuca to reach them. Numerous small communities along the coast could be destroyed. The likelihood of such a fault-generated tsunami in that location is uncertain.

Alaska has no monopoly on destructive earthquakes. Wherever mountain ranges are being uplifted, serious earthquakes are common. India has suffered many devastating earthquakes. At the beginning of this century an earthquake there took an estimated 25,000 lives. One in 1935 claimed 56,000. In 1950 about 5,000 more died. These disturbances and others occurred in the foothills of the Himalaya Mountains and are evidence of the forces currently elevating those mountains. Rocks formed of sediment once deposited in a lowland are now being thrust high into the air, forming the mountain peaks of Everest and the adjoining ranges. Wherever the population is great, the buildings fragile, and the disturbances severe, the loss of life is likely to be extreme. China, for example, often suffers many casualties. One earthquake-induced landslide in 1920 took 200,000 lives, but the worst on record, also in China, occurred in 1556 when 830,000 died. Closer to home, two severe earthquakes struck Mexico City in 1985, and more than 7,000 people perished. The city is located on the flat surface of a former lake bed, and the damage done there serves as another example of how earthquakes are more severe in the soft sediments of filled land.

Volcanic Mountains of the West

Mount Saint Helens, the volcanic peak that erupted in 1980, provided a spectacular display, along with considerable scientific information about mountain building. The mountain lies in the Cascade Range of Washington State, about 40 miles north of Portland, Oregon, and the Columbia River, and its eruption has provided a significant view of the mountain-building forces now at work in the West.

Mount Saint Helens was a quiet, snowcapped peak plainly visible from the main highway between Seattle, Washington, and Portland, Oregon. The tall white cone towered above the forests of the Cascade Range. There, among the towering evergreen trees that stood beside picturesque Spirit Lake at the base of the mountain, was a quiet location far from the blaring cacophony of city life.

Spirit Lake got its name from local Indians who found that the quiet waters would occasionally become turbulent, though without wind. It seemed the spirits were causing the turbulence. In a five-year period during the 1920s there were several reports of fishermen in small boats on the otherwise quiet surface who were suddenly caught in turbulent water and their boats overturned. On two occasions men drowned. No further incidents have since been reported. Either the spirits became more tranquil, or, as volcanologists insist, the turbulence was evidence of deep-seated volcanic activity

Pre-eruption, the lower slope of the mountain featured the Goat Point lava flow. Other geological finds included lumps of pumice. The pumice and lava together indicate the mountain is a composite cone, developed through alternating periods of quietly erupting lava flows, as indicated by the dark, almost black rock of Goat Point, and explosive eruptions, which hurled clouds of fine, light-colored pumice into the air, some of it falling back to build the towering volcanic peak. The light-colored pumice thus provides evidence of a more spectacular eruption. The chunks of pumice are full of air holes formed by gases blasting through molten rock as it is hurled into the air. Unlike other rocks, pumice is so full of air holes, it will float on water.

The dark basaltic lava in the foreground here indicates a gentle eruption occurred in the past, before the great eruption of Mount Saint Helens in 1980. But some eruptions were violent, as indicated by the pumice, a more resistant type of magma, in the background.

The two kinds of rock on such volcanic peaks are significant. The eruption of dark basaltic rock is less violent, for the basalt flows more freely, as in the Hawaii volcanoes. In contrast, the light-colored rock is more viscous and, like cold molasses, will not flow freely. Consequently such felsitic magma, as it is known, resists flowing until pressures mount sufficiently to blast through the resisting rock. The presence of two types of rock on Mount Saint Helens indicates that the molten rock surging up from deep underground was not always the same.

In April of 1980, the tranquillity of the quiet north slope of Mount Saint Helens was interrupted as the mountain bulged upward, then blasted forth in a violent eruption that carried away the entire mountaintop, leaving behind an empty crater. Pumice formed towering clouds above the now hollow mountain. The sky was obscured by a thick sheet of pumice, often termed ash, that was much like smoke from a fire. The ash drifted in all directions, but mostly toward the northeast with the prevailing winds.

Closer to the mountain, the force of the blast downed the gigantic trees of the virgin forest and left Spirit Lake a desolate mud hole. A lumber company came in to salvage what it could of the felled timber, and biologists began a continuing study of the destroyed ecosystem and the gradual reestablishment of plants and animals in the desolate region. The mountain itself was scarcely recognizable, having become a hollow crater.

The Cascades photographed from the side of Mount Saint Helens, taken before the eruption. A portion of Spirit Lake at the foot of the mountain is visible in the photograph.

Volcanologists—geologists who study volcanic activity—were fascinated by the opportunity to follow closely the lingering activity that was building a rounded dome within the crater. Other volcanic peaks of the Cascade Range are said to be dormant, some possibly extinct, but nobody is quite sure. Lingering activity is evident in Mount Hood and Mount Baker. These and others could become active again.

As the North American continent drifts westward, overriding the heavy rocks of the ocean bed, rocks deep within the Earth's crust experience high pressures and are heated, creating gases that separate from the now molten rock and escape through fissures above. On occasion, as the pressures mount, both the gases and molten rock escape, erupting as volcanoes—or dissipating the heat by way of lesser disturbances, such as the geysers and mud pots of Yellowstone Park. The rocks of the ocean bed that descend into the Earth when overridden may carry with them lighter felsitic rock material, such as sands from the beaches. When the felsitic rock is ejected, it becomes the pumice formed in an explosive volcanic eruption.

In Alaska, where the ocean bed is drifting northward against the land, mountain building is more evident and volcanic activity more frequent. There too the ocean bed is being subducted, not only uplifting the adjoining continent but also carrying rock from ocean bed and shore deep under the surface of the land. The subducted rock forms magma under pressure, which occasionally is forced upward through fissures in volcanic eruptions. A recent example is the eruption of Mount Redoubt in December 1989. Redoubt is in plain sight from across Cook Inlet, a short distance west of Anchorage. Numerous other volcanic peaks are located along the Alaska Peninsula and in the Aleutian Islands.

One prominent volcanic area on the peninsula has been established as the Katmai National Park, 290 miles from Anchorage. The eruption of Katmai in 1912 was one of the most violent anywhere in the world. Because few, if any, people were nearby, no lives are known to have been lost. Violent earthquakes preceding the eruption may have frightened any inhabitants out of the area. Loud explosions accompanying the eruption were heard far away as clouds of ash rose to obscure the sky. Later inspection found native villages deserted and ash as deep as 15 feet covering the immediate area. Ash a foot deep covered everything for many miles around. The volume of rock ejected in the explosion was immense. After the eruption, what was left of the mountain collapsed to form a large empty crater called a caldera, which has since filled with water to become a lake. Subsequently, new volcanic peaks developed and erupted again in 1931 and 1950. The cataclysmic explosion of 1912 left a volcanic area that has become known as the "Valley of Ten Thousand Smokes."

Although extremely violent, the Katmai eruption was not unique in the region. Just to the northeast in the Alaska Range is the Lake Clark National Park and Preserve, which includes not only Redoubt but also Iliamna, another active volcano. On the Alaska Peninsula about 130 miles southwest of Katmai is the Aniakchak National Monument, which contains another huge collapsed volcanic caldera. A new volcanic cone has risen within that caldera, and twice that new peak has erupted.

To the southwest, on the long Alaska Peninsula and the raggedly extending Aleutian Islands, numerous volcanoes are located close to the coast where the oceanic rocks are pressing forward and dipping down under the lighter rocks of the continent. These Alaskan volcanoes, and lofty mountains farther inland, provide an ongoing demonstration of how mountains in the past were uplifted and how others are still being elevated.

In Hawaii, the Kilauea volcano erupts frequently. The dark basaltic rock of the underlying ocean bed rises and flows rather freely so eruptions there are seldom hazardous, except for buildings engulfed and destroyed in lava flows. Interestingly, the Hawaiian Islands are a chain of extinct volcanoes. As the ocean bed gradually drifted northward, it passed over a "hot spot" where molten rock was rising from the depths. A volcanic island was formed slowly, as the movement of the ocean bed carried the island northward, while another island began to form over the same rising plume of lava. The active volcano, Kilauea, is at the southern end of the island chain. That southern island is the largest of the islands, formed by three massive volcanoes whose lava fields merged to form a single island.

Volcanic eruptions are frequent and often highly destructive in Central America. The westward drift of the land overriding the descending rocks of the ocean bed is responsible for the eruptions there, as in Hawaii and Alaska. In South America, the volcanic activity is likely to be destructive, largely because fragile houses are poorly located and unable to withstand the power of either an earthquake or a volcanic eruption. In 1985, for example, a long-dormant volcano in Colombia erupted, killing 22,800 people and destroying much property. In 1943 a new volcano erupted in what had been a quiet Mexican cornfield. A stream of lava engulfed the nearby village of Parícutin, completely destroying everything in its path. A long dormant Mexican volcano, El Chichon, in 1982, emitted vast amounts of ash, destroying crops and fields while taking the lives of more than 20 people.

Perhaps the greatest ever of all the volcanic mountains in the Cascade Range, Mount Mazama in southern Oregon, no longer exists. About 7,700 years ago the mountain was destroyed in a violent eruption. The entire mountain was blown away, leaving only an empty crater, a *caldera*. The eruption was similar to that of Mount Saint Helens, except that this mountain was taller and more massive. The cavity left behind has filled with water, forming Crater Lake, now a national park. The lake is almost circular, with an average width of about five miles, and a depth of 1,932 feet, making it the nation's deepest. After the gigantic eruption, whatever was left of the mountain collapsed into the inner cavity. Although the lake is very deep, the caldera is by no means filled, for the rim that marks the base of the former mountain stands far above the level of the water.

Ash from the eruption spread with the wind northward into Canada and eastward into Montana, accumulating in depths sufficient to be plainly discernible even today. Close to the mountain the compacted pumice is as much as 20 feet deep in banks by the roadside. At the time of the eruption, Indians lived in the area, as evidenced by spear points and other Indian artifacts that have been found covered and preserved by the ash.

As in other eruptions, oceanic rock was overrun by the westward drift of the American continent. Under intense pressure, these rocks became molten and broke through to the surface. Rocks at the base of Mount Mazama are similar in composition to those of the ocean bed. Later the molten rock changed to become the more resistant dacite, which contains more quartz, as if derived from beach sands subducted along with the rocks of the ocean bed.

Lava Fields of the West

Between the Cascade Range and the Rocky Mountains lies a broad region of lava fields extending from near the Canadian border south into much of Utah and Nevada as well as northeastern California. As the North American continent drifted westward over the bed of the Pacific Ocean, much of the dark oceanic rock erupted onto the surface. Flowing rather freely, the hot rock spread out over the surface with little violence, much

The Athabasca Glacier in western Canada. To the left are tributary glaciers between glaciated peaks. Beyond the main glacier is an edge of the great Columbia Ice Field. In the foreground is an outwash plain and glacial lake.

as lava does in Hawaii. This vast expanse of black rock is one of the two largest lava fields in the world; the other covers a broad area of India and is associated with the mountain-building forces that built the great Himalaya Mountain Range.

The Columbia River rises in the Rocky Mountains of Canada, fed by the meltwater of the Columbia ice fields. From British Columbia the water flows down through the scenic foothills of the mountains across the border into the United States. The Columbia then follows a somewhat circuitous course southward across the lowland lava fields of eastern Washington, finally curving westward through the Cascade Range to the Pacific Ocean at Astoria, Oregon. Explorers and pioneers found the Columbia Gorge a better route to the west coast than climbing up and over the mountains. Those pioneers, impressed with the rapids, or cascades, used that term in reference to the mountains themselves, and thus the entire mountain range became known as the Cascades. Apparently, the river followed its westward course before the mountains were elevated and was able to maintain that course by cutting them down as rapidly as they rose. The walls of the gorge cut by the river now expose many layers of lava, one lava flow upon another. The continual presence of rapids in the mountain area indicates that the river is still cutting its channel through the flows.

As a stream flows over the rocks of a cascade or waterfall, the rocks gradually break away, lowering the stream bed. The falls or rapids thus retreat upstream, and eventually a smooth channel is established. The Columbia has not completed that process; now, with power dams along the river, the process has been halted or at least retarded.

The Cascades are built largely of the same basaltic rock as the adjoining, depressed lava fields, which were folded down by the same pressures that uplifted the mountains. As more lava oozed out onto the lowland, the additional weight of the rock caused the land to sink further. Since molten basalt flows quite freely, the eruptions from numerous fissures were

The Yellowstone River is cutting into the flat surface of the Rocky Mountain Plateau. Stream valleys are normally V-shaped, but they may become wider as rocks slide down the valley walls. Yellowstone Falls were formed where harder rock was encounterd.

seldom violent. Instead, the lava spread quietly over broad areas, forming lava beds about as deep as the mountains are high.

During the most recent Ice Age, tongues of ice extending southward blocked the normal drainage of the Columbia River in the northern mountains. One such extension of glacial ice blocked the Clark Fork River at a point close to the present Pend Oreille Lake in northern Idaho, northeast of present-day Spokane. With the drainage blocked, the water backed up behind the dam, forming a huge lake that extended past Missoula almost to the continental divide at Helena in Montana. When the lake filled to overflowing, the obstruction broke, and an immense flood plunged through the opening down into the lava fields below.

The swift water cut a network of deep channels in the hard, black rock, forming what are now called scablands, with individual channels known as coulees. The largest of these is the Grand Coulee, now occupied by the Columbia River. The Grand Coulee has been dammed to create a huge reservoir for generating electric power and to maintain water for irrigating this otherwise dry region. Now Yakima and Wenatchee are surrounded by extensive orchards, and the inexpensive electricity generated has been a strong stimulus for industrial development.

Also noteworthy in the lava fields of eastern Washington is Ginkgo State Park at the eastern edge of the Cascade Range, overlooking the Columbia River, where the stumps of petrified ginkgo trees stand in their original positions. Only the stumps were preserved, a result of lava having covered only the lower portions of the trees. Minerals from the lava replaced the wood as it decayed.

Ginkgo trees are quite distinctive. They were common during the Jurassic Period's Mesozoic Era, when huge dinosaurs were predominant, but were thought to be extinct like the dinosaurs. They were later found growing in the Orient, maintained at temples in Japan and China. The trees were then reintroduced into America, with many being planted along the streets of New York City, where they are now in a sense living fossils. But in Washington's Petrified Forest they remain as true fossils.

The lava found in the mountains indicates that the lava fields were spreading before the Cascades rose, which means the lava fields once extended farther west, where the mountains stand today. Even now the area covered by lava is very broad. The Snake River, beginning at the foot of the Grand Teton Mountains adjoining Yellowstone National Park, flows westward across the continuous expanse of lava fields in southern Idaho up to Oregon. There the entrenched course is known as Hell's Canyon, now a national recreation area. It is about as deep and wide as the Grand Canyon yet gets less attention. The Salmon River also has a deep canyon in the great lava fields. The lava here is sufficiently recent to appear fresh and unspoiled. An especially fine area of lava beds has been preserved as the Craters of the Moon National Monument, located north of Twin Falls and west of Idaho Falls. These and other falls of the Snake River, along with the comparatively fresh lava, indicate recent crustal disturbances.

Eastern Oregon, likewise, is largely covered by effusive lava flows. In the dry lands east of the Cascades some sagebrush and other dryland shrubs have gained a foothold. Near the Idaho border, where the land has

The Snake River in the lava fields of southeast Washington State. Settlers passed along here on their way to the Oregon Territory. This river traverses the vast lava fields east of the Cascade Range.

16

Crater Lake in southern Oregon is all that remains of a huge volcanic eruption. Here a portion of the rim of the former mountain can be seen. The island is a cinder cone built by lingering volcanism after the main eruption.

been uplifted to form the Blue Mountains, pines and other evergreens have grown, as in the west where evergreen forests have developed at the border of lava fields and the foothills of the Cascades.

At the edge of the Deschutes National Forest is a noteworthy area known as Lavalands, where lingering volcanic activity has formed what is known as the Newberry "volcano." Lava ceased flowing about 10,000 years ago, when the pressure from below subsided and the interior collapsed, leaving a high rim surrounding a cavity—a caldera similar to that of Crater Lake. In this case the caldera is divided into two lakes rather than one, as at the national park farther south. Near the Newberry volcano are many small cinder cones built by escaping gases, which rose through still molten rock while the eruptions were coming to a gradual halt. The caldera itself is roughly circular, about five miles in diameter. In the surrounding lava fields are large tunnels where hot rock continued to flow after the surrounding lava had cooled and hardened. As the last of the still-molten lava flowed through, an empty conduit remained in the already congealed field of lava. These lava tunnels vary in size, but one is more than half a mile long and in places as wide and large as a room. These lava fields created many interesting sights. Where a lava flow dammed the McKenzie River we now have Clear Lake. Trees that stood in that valley have now become a fossilized forest, visible beneath the surface of the lake. As the wood decayed, minerals from the water soaked in to form replicas of the original trees.

At the north end of the lava fields, in a wilderness area about 40 miles south of Mount Hood, stands Mount Jefferson. Jefferson is a well-shaped peak almost as tall as Mount Hood and consisting of lava and extruded pumice. Also prominent in the midst of the lava fields of central Oregon are the Three Sisters, each a little more than 10,000 feet high. The line of volcanic peaks has helped to make central Oregon a year-round recreational area. In addition to more than 100 cinder cones, this volcanic area includes the eroded spires of such prominences as Thielson, Washington, Union Peak, and Three Fingered Jack. Other conspicuous prominences include Batchlor Butte, Broken Top, Odell Butte, Cowhorn Mountain, Walker Mountain, Pumice Butte, Maiden Peak, the Twins, and countless others. Not to be overlooked are the limestone caverns of Oregon Caves National Monument, near the coast in southern Oregon.

Across the border in northeastern California is Lava Beds National Monument with a broad view of lava fields. The monument is well named, for its basaltic lava forms a bare surface of hard, black rock, little changed since it rose from the depths more than 1,000 years ago. As one mass of rock cooled and hardened, the next surge of lava overran the earlier one and broke it into fragments, which then became engulfed as portions of a larger mass termed *breccia.* Wherever gases escaped through the molten mass, bubble holes remain in the hardened lava, somewhat like the tiny holes in a loaf of bread baked in an oven. Wherever the hot lava flowed over a pool of water, steam escaped through the molten rock, forming an abundance of air holes. Such rock is termed *vesicular basalt,* or *scoria.* Lava tunnels and cinder cones abound in these lava beds.

Mount Lassen in California had experienced the most recent volcanic eruption in the West prior to Mount St. Helens. Lassen is located along a fault line at the northern end of the Sierra Nevada, south of Mount Shasta and the Lava Beds National Monument.

A short distance to the south of this national monument is Medicine Lake sitting in what was originally a volcano but is now a broad caldera surrounded by a rim of rock with sloping sides. Following a catastrophic eruption and collapse, a number of lingering eruptions in the surrounding area built cinder cones, or in some cases masses of volcanic glass, or obsidian. A massive example is known as Glass Mountain. This lava is glass without crystals. Smaller broken pieces are transparent, but larger chunks appear black. These lava fields of northeastern California are part of a continuous expanse extending from near the Canadian border southward into Nevada and Utah.

Glass Mountain is a short way south of Mount Lassen. Its volcanic glass component, obsidian, contrasts with the basaltic rock of Lassen, which contains more quartz, indicating a different sort of magma.

Scenic Wonders of the Pacific Northwest

In the Far West there are innumerable scenic views. The view from Mount Saint Helens National Volcanic Monument is especially commanding. The highest, most massive volcanic mountain of the Cascades, Mount Rainier, southeast of Seattle, is plainly visible from there. Mount Whitney in the Sierra Nevada, officially recognized as the highest peak in the 48 states, is less than eight feet higher, which in mountain terms is virtually nothing at all. The two are quite different, however. Whitney, being solid rock, elevated with the Sierra Nevada, and Rainier, which is volcanic, was built from eruptions of lava and pumice. Mount Rainier has not erupted recently, though steam has occasionally issued from the summit and mountain climbers have noted that the craters there are quite hot. The occasional earthquakes accompanied by rumbling sounds with concurrent avalanches of snow, mud, and rock indicate that Rainier is dormant but not extinct.

The best views of a neighboring mountain, Mount Adams, can be obtained from the east, beyond the Cascades and south of Mount Rainier. Mount Baker, in the Cascades 15 miles from the Canadian border, was threatening to erupt in 1975, but nothing serious happened. A resort area on the side of the mountain provides a spectacular view of the glacier on the adjoining Mount Shuksan, which is reported to be part of a terrane developed elsewhere but added to the North American continent (see chapter 10).

Mount Rainier, with the Nisqually Glacier on the right, is the tallest, most massive of the volcanic mountains in the Cascade Range. It is dormant, but not extinct.

Glacier Peak, another volcanic mountain similar to Mount Baker and almost as high, is not as well known to the public. Somewhat remote and deep in a pristine area of the Broad Cascades, it is not visible from the well-traveled highways. Splendid views can be obtained from interior roads, but more intimate contact is available only to hikers.

Within the northern reaches of the Cascades in British Columbia are the distinctive volcanic peaks of Mount Garibaldi. Although emitting an abundance of ash and flaming rock when it erupted during the Ice Age, the twin peaks are made of lava, now hardened rock. Garibaldi is the featured attraction of a provincial park a short way inland and 40 miles north of Vancouver.

Mount Hood is a prominent sight from Portland, Oregon, especially from Terwilleger Heights. For closer views, the Mount Hood Loop Highway is ideal. Mount Adams and what remains of Mount Saint Helens are visible in the north. The Loop Highway begins on the east side of Portland and provides not only good views but also access to resort areas on the side of Mount Hood itself. On the return to Portland, the loop is completed by joining the Columbia River Highway near Hood River, which then passes the cascades where the Bridge of the Gods is reputed to have been located, also the large Bonneville Dam and power station, as well as Bridal Veil Falls and Multnomah Falls. Crown Point provides a sensational view of a broad panorama from high on the canyon wall almost straight down to the river far below.

To visit Olympic National Park, one good route is from Olympia, the state capital, north along the west side of Puget Sound. Another way is to cross the sound by ferry from Seattle to Bremerton. A huge naval shipyard is located at Bremerton. For those who wish, arrangements can be made to tour the shipyards, also the U.S.S. *Missouri* docked there. The peace treaty with Japan was signed aboard the *Missouri*. Another route north from Tacoma likewise provides good views of Puget Sound.

Geologists tell us that long ago Puget Sound was a network of valleys with streams merging to flow westward through what is now the Strait of Juan de Fuca. As the mountain ranges on each side were uplifted, the valleys of Puget Sound were depressed and inundated. In addition to the downward folding of the Puget Basin during the Ice Age, glaciers scoured the mountainsides and carried great amounts of clay, sand, and stone into the lowland. The additional weight further depressed the region. Geologists term Puget Sound and the strait that separates the state from Canada an extensive system of drowned valleys.

From the Visitor Center in Port Angeles, north of Bremerton, a good road leads up to a resort area high in the Olympic Mountains at Hurricane Ridge. A short walk out along the ridge provides a splendid view of the mountains. The more or less uniform height of the ridges suggests that comparatively flat land was uplifted to the present elevation of about a mile above sea level, with Mount Olympus highest at 7,965 feet. Heavy rainfall and snow compacted to form glaciers have shaped the mountains, carving deep valleys into the uplifted land. Standing on Hurricane Ridge and looking out across the Olympics rewards with an impressive sight. It is also revealing to notice the sparse vegetation along the ridge in comparison to the heavy timber and thick underbrush, which thrive at lower levels. There are still a number of active glaciers in these mountains, especially on Mount Olympus, but most of these are visible only from the west, the direction of the prevailing winds that bring the snow and rain.

From Port Angeles a scenic highway proceeds westward along the foot of the mountains, with the broad Strait of Juan de Fuca on the opposite side. Along the way, beautiful Crescent Lake will invite travelers to tarry, and swimming in a pool of naturally warm water at the Solduc Hot Springs may also be inviting. Hot water seeps up from below into the pool, which is fine until someone in the pool steps onto one of the hot spots, which will induce the bather to step lively. The hot water rising into the pool means that hot rocks are not far below the surface. Those hot rocks suggest that mountain building in the Olympics is not far back in the past.

As the scenic highway nears the ocean and bends toward the south, a spur leads out to the Indian Reservation at Neah Bay. Travelers who feel energetic and in need of some mild exercise can walk the rest of the way along a short, level trail through the woods to Cape Flattery, the extreme northwest corner of the 48 states, where the Strait of Juan de Fuca meets the Pacific Ocean. This view is well worth the effort. There it is evident how the pounding waves can cut into the rocks along a shore.

Heading south along the coast at the foot of the mountains will provide good views of the temperate rain forest, with its dense underbrush and abundant moss hanging from the trees. The highest annual rainfall in North America is in those mountains. A short distance beyond the town of Forks, at the Huh River, a road leads back into the rain forest itself.

Historically the mouth of the Columbia River at Astoria was a center for fur traders and missionaries, and for those who fish it still is a lure. Astoria was the terminus for the Lewis and Clark Expedition into the wilderness of the West. Now, a bit farther south, Seaside has a long-standing reputation as the favorite beach of Oregonians. Just beyond is Cannon Beach, which some say is the most beautiful in the world outside the tropics. Cannon Beach features many sea stacks, which are rock prominences just offshore. Where the land has risen, stormy waves have cut back the shore, with resistant rock formations left standing. Rocky banks along the shore eventually may become sea stacks as the process continues. Noteworthy farther down the coast is the Oregon Dunes National Recreation Area. In Oregon, as in Washington, the climate is mild—comparatively warm in the winter and cool in the summer. The prevailing westerly winds off the Pacific Ocean bring the Pacific Northwest what is known as a *marine climate.*

In the Pacific Northwest near the Canadian border a large wilderness area has been designated a national park, as have Mount Rainier and Crater Lake. Since the great eruption, Mount Saint Helens has been declared a national volcanic monument. These, along with state parks and other featured sites, make the Pacific Northwest a wonderland, especially attractive to travelers with sufficient insight to appreciate them.

2

MOUNTAINS' INFLUENCE ON LIFE

Mountains have a profound effect on the weather, as well as on living conditions for plants, animals, and people. The rainiest place in North America is on the Pacific Coast, in the Olympic Mountains, where a weather station has recorded rainfall six times as heavy as the annual 40 inches typical of New York, Boston, Washington, D.C., and other East Coast locations. Throughout the Pacific Northwest, many locations receive abundant rain. One town at the foot of the Cascades is appropriately named "Mossyrock." Because of the humid air, moss grows profusely on the rocks and trees there. Strands of moss droop down from the limbs of trees like fringes of lace.

A facetious expression heard in and about Seattle is that "summer came on a Saturday last year, but I was out of town and missed it." Another frequently heard remark refers to the light rain as "Oregon mist—it missed Oregon and hit Washington." The entire region has a reputation of being perpetually rainy. But this is not the whole truth. For example, the small town Quilcene is located across Puget Sound from Seattle, at the eastern side of the Olympic Mountains. Situated at the foot of the mountains, only a few miles from the heights where the rainfall is extremely heavy, Quilcene is quite dry, with an annual rainfall of only about 15 inches, approximately a third that of Boston or New York. Quilcene is in the so-called rain shadow of the Olympics. Even in Seattle the yearly rainfall is slightly less than that of Boston, New York, or Philadelphia (39.32 inches compared with 40.43 inches, 41.42 inches, and 44.61 inches). So why does the Pacific Northwest have a reputation for constant rain?

In Seattle, as throughout the region, the prevailing westerly winds come off the Pacific Ocean, bringing moisture. Ocean water fluctuates only slightly in temperature with the seasons so that during the winter the land is colder than the temperate winds off the water. As we know, heat causes evaporation. Conversely, when cooled, the moisture of humid air will condense as rain or some other form of precipitation.

On the east side of the Cascade Range, prevailing winds from the west cause the air to become compressed and heated as it descends to lower levels, resulting in a drying effect, leaving vegetation stunted, lacking moisture.

Accordingly, warm moist winds off the Pacific Ocean tend to bring rain when the land is cold. Aberdeen, Washington, located on the coast, has about 90 inches of rain each year, which is twice that of cities on the East Coast. During the winter, as incoming winds are cooled, winter rains in Aberdeen are frequent and heavy.

The Olympic Mountains are just to the north of Aberdeen. In those mountains the prevailing winds are forced to rise to higher levels. As anyone who has traveled in the mountains knows, air is cooler at higher elevations. So the prevailing westerly winds there are cooled not only by the winter temperatures but also as they rise to higher elevations. Consequently, rainfall is heavy in the Olympic Mountains, too.

MOUNTAINS' INFLUENCE ON LIFE

After passing over the mountains, the air tends to sink to lower levels where the land is not as cold. Because of the higher temperatures at lower levels, the effect is reversed. Increasing warmth causes water to evaporate, rather than to condense as rain. For that reason, Quilcene—just east of the mountains—is quite dry.

Seattle also is east of the Olympics, although not as close to the mountains. Yet rainfall there is not heavy, despite what people say. As the prevailing winds rise to pass over the Olympics, moisture condenses to form clouds, and these clouds persist, obscuring the sun as they drift eastward high above the city. The general effect is many overcast days in Seattle. Often those clouds do yield a bit of rain, a light mist. Though Seattle may get many rainy days, the rains are light, and the total rainfall less than that of East Coast cities—all because of Seattle's location in a

In the highlands west of San Francisco, vegetation is abundant where winds rise to pass over the mountains, but scarce where the winds are no longer rising.

27

valley between two mountain ranges, the Olympics of the Coast Range and the Cascades farther inland.

Since water temperature fluctuates only slightly (due to a high specific heat), winds off the Pacific Ocean keep the West Coast mild. In Seattle, the coldest temperatures in January average only 33 degrees and likewise in the summer—when the westerly winds are comparatively cool, the highest temperatures average only 75 degrees. So the region is seldom very hot or very cold, maintaining a moderate "marine climate." Moreover, summer is a dry season there, with summer rainfall averages of only four-tenths of an inch, whereas on the East Coast the average is 10 times as great for the summer months. Since summer temperatures are mild, thunderstorms seldom occur in those months out West, but do rain down on eastern cities. Even along the coastal lowlands at the foot of the Olympics, in the midst of dense vegetation characteristic of a temperate rain forest, the summers are so dry that great depths of dry dust can be seen along the roads.

Why is the region dry in the summer? During those months the land is warmer than the ocean. Accordingly, the incoming winds are heated slightly, and heating has a drying effect, keeping the summers dry and mild. However, because of the mountains, the other nine months are the rainy season for most of the region. Even in the winter, temperatures seldom drop sufficiently to bring snow, except in the mountains. On those rare occasions when Seattle does get heavy snow, traffic is snarled until snow plows can be brought down from the mountains, where snow is more common.

The Cascade Range divides the state of Washington into two quite different regions, east and west. The Cascades continue south through Oregon, and the east side there likewise is much different from the west. But the mountains forming the divide are not quite so steep in Oregon; hence the regions are not as sharply delineated. Highways leading up into the Cascades from the west are steep, forcing many automobiles to climb in second gear. On each side of the road is a dense forest of fir, spruce, and hemlock. As a result of the heavy rainfall, underbrush is thick, making walking about in the forest beneath the tall timber possible only along trails kept open by deer and other animals.

At the summit of a mountain pass, there is an abrupt change. Instead of grinding away in second gear climbing up, motorists begin using their brakes going down. Instead of tall spruce, hemlock, and fir, visitors find short pine trees. Moreover, the pines stand far apart with little if any brush beneath the trees. Pine needles cover the otherwise bare ground. On the west side of the mountains such open spaces are found only in parks where the underbrush has been cleared. Continuing down the mountain, the motorist finds trees even farther apart and still shorter. It seems that pines can tolerate a drier climate than can the trees on the west side. With rainfall becoming still more limited farther down the mountain, even stunted pines become scarce, and eventually there are none—nothing but scattered brush and clumps of dry grass. At the foot of the mountain, vegetation is nonexistent, except for greasewood and other desert plants. There are many barren spaces with nothing but sand and solid rock. At the foot of the mountains is a desert with rainfall as low as five to 10 inches a year. Farther from the mountains the lack of rain is less extreme yet still severely limited. Farming is possible at Yakima and other locations east of the mountains only because of irrigation with water from the Columbia River, which flows through the desert from the mountains farther north.

Briefly stated, Yakima is in the rain shadow of the Cascades. On the west side of the mountains, moist winds off the Pacific Ocean are cooled as they rise to higher elevations where the air pressure is less, the air expands, and the expansion causes cooling. Cooling then causes the water vapor to condense as rain or snow. (Note that the spray from a can of hair spray is quite cool due to expansion, and the can itself becomes cool, even though the can and its contents are at room temperature.) The cooling causes the clouds often seen about mountaintops. If the cooling is sufficient, the tiny drops of water in a cloud will become larger and will fall as rain. If the temperature is low enough, the vapor will freeze as it condenses and snow will fall. Because of the low temperatures at high elevations, snow is common in the mountains.

On the east side of the mountains, in contrast, the air tends to settle to a lower level where the air pressure is greater. Air pressure is due to the weight of the air pressing down from above. At lower levels there is more air above; hence the pressure is greater. With greater pressure the air is compressed, which causes it to become heated, and the heating has a drying effect. Thus winds that descend the east side of the Cascades are heated by compression, making the region there warm and dry.

The Cascades provide a vivid example of the way mountains affect the climate and the vegetation dependent upon that climate. In turn, the climate and the vegetation both have a direct effect on the kinds of animals that can live in the region. Accordingly, both the vegetation and the animal life are to a large extent different, not only on the two sides of the Cascades but also different from what is common beyond the Rocky Mountains in the East. Robins, for example, are orange-breasted in the East but red in the West. Also, a variety of snakes are common in the East, whereas in the Pacific Northwest there is only the nonpoisonous garter snake.

The effects of mountains on rainfall so vividly exemplified by the Cascades are manifest elsewhere to varying degrees. Denver is a good example. Although the "Mile High City" is often assumed to be in the Rocky Mountains, it is actually on the Great Plains close to the foot of the mountains. Being on the eastern, leeward side, the rainfall is light, only a little more than 15 inches annually, and would be even less except for occasional storms off the Gulf of Mexico. Cheyenne, Wyoming, also on the Great Plains east of the mountains, has even less rain than Denver. Other good examples are plentiful throughout the very dry High Plains region east of the Rocky Mountains. Still more impressive in their aridity are the Mojave Desert and Death Valley, east of the high and abrupt Sierra Nevada.

Less extreme examples can be found anywhere the prevailing winds pass over even a small hill. For instance, in Ohio where trees were being planted on a rounded hilltop to establish a tree farm, the small slope made a big difference. On the southwest side thick grass choked out the seedlings. The year-old plants had to be replaced several times, because the grass grew so fast that the tiny trees were crowded out. Beyond the crest of the hill on the drier north slope there was no such problem.

Washington is known as the "Evergreen State"; the frequent light rains there keep everything green despite the dry summers. Nevertheless, that slogan applies only in the west, where most of the people live, for on the other side of the mountains the land is quite dry. At least it is dry until near the Idaho border, where the foothills of the Rocky Mountains begin. There at Spokane the slightly increased elevation brings the annual precipitation up to a meager 17½ inches—in contrast to the more than 67 inches in the "Sunshine State" at Miami.

In addition to the obvious regional influence of mountains on the climate and on life in general, there may be even more profound, far-reaching effects. About a million years ago the climate throughout the Northern Hemisphere turned markedly colder. As a result much snow fell and became compacted as ice. In central Canada huge mountains of ice accumulated, and the ice gradually spread southward as far as Long Island in New York and the Ohio Valley in the Midwest.

Before the Ice Age, conditions throughout the world ordinarily were hot and humid with abundant rainfall, much like conditions in the tropics today. Geological evidence in the rocks leaves little doubt that balmy weather prevailed. So why the big change? Nobody knows for sure. Perhaps there were variations in the heat from the sun. Some stars are variable in the radiation they emit, and not as uniform as we assume our sun to be. Irregularities in the Earth's orbit around the sun have been suggested as one possible explanation. Now that geologists have become aware of plate tectonics, the movement of continents on the surface of the Earth, it has been suggested that the continents have drifted farther from the warmth of the equator to more northerly locations.

In these last million years, many huge mountain ranges have been uplifted, including the Cascades, Sierra Nevada, and the Coast Range of the American West. The Rocky Mountains along with the broad Colorado Plateau were in existence earlier but have continued to be mountainous. The Andes of South America, the Himalayas with the vast Tibetan Plateau in Asia, and the Alps of Europe all have been elevated to unusual heights in comparatively recent times. It now seems likely these extensive mountain ranges were largely responsible for the climatic changes of the Ice Age.

It has been suggested that the mountain ranges and their associated plateaus divert the prevailing winds and thus alter previous weather conditions. Winds diverted northward eventually carry cold air into middle latitudes. Cold air from the broad surface of the Tibetan Plateau or the Colorado Plateau eventually sinks to lower elevations. Before the mountains were uplifted, lowlands in those regions were a source of much warmer air to be distributed by the prevailing winds.

When coal, oil, or other fuels burn, oxygen from the air combines with the fuel, releasing heat while producing carbon dioxide. In recent years concern has developed that with the world's increasing use of such fuels as sources of energy, the greater abundance of carbon dioxide in the atmosphere may act as a blanket, allowing radiation from the sun to penetrate but trapping the resulting heat and causing worldwide temperatures to rise. In contrast, during the Ice Age, with the uplift of mountains, many fresh surfaces of rock were exposed to weathering. During weathering of rocks, considerable carbon dioxide combines with minerals in the rocks. Much carbon dioxide is removed from the atmosphere, allowing heat to escape into outer space and reducing surface temperatures. It has been suggested that such conditions could have been one large factor initiating the Ice Age. Thus in several ways the uplift of mountain ranges with their extensive plateaus could have been influential in bringing about the Ice Age. Clearly, mountains are far more than spectacular sights.

Marking Time by the Mountains

Mountains are very old, some older than others, but none have been there forever. It is difficult to think of some mountains as growing, others as having become old and worn. Yet like ourselves, mountains do grow and change; the changes simply take longer. Where the Rocky Mountains are today was once a muddy lowland. The Appalachians are even older and badly worn down. When those mountains were young, millions of years ago, there was no Atlantic Ocean. Africa was tightly pressed against what is now our east coast. In contrast, the Cascades along the Pacific Coast are still quite young, still growing. Spectacular evidence of such youthful development was provided in 1980 when Mount Saint Helens erupted.

Mountain building can be catastrophic but not always so. The mountains of the Sierra Nevada, for example, are growing taller a little at a time. The Appalachians, too, are changing as streams cut away the highlands. Those mountains have gone through immense changes. Great thrust faults can be seen where pressure from the east caused the rocks to break and slide inland, or to bend and fold upward, thereby building the mountains. Movement along those great fault lines no doubt caused the tremors of earthquakes, some even more severe than any in California today. Volcanoes erupted throughout the Appalachians from Maine to Alabama as the mountains were being uplifted. Lava from the eruptions is still there as evidence of what happened.

Before the development of geological science, it was commonly believed the Earth was only about 6,000 years old. But with newer knowledge the estimates have been extended repeatedly. Now the commonly accepted age of the Earth is about 4½ billion years, but even that may be inaccurate. When geological time is stated in years, the numbers are merely estimates. As explained in a later chapter, the estimates today are more accurate than in the past, but the numbers are still so general and so large they tend to be meaningless. In contrast, when occurrences of the distant past are expressed in terms of geological eras and periods, the emphasis is on relationships, and thus more meaningful. The dinosaur tracks in the Connecticut Valley, for example, were made in the Triassic Period, which is the first period after the Appalachians were uplifted; accordingly, the mountains on each side of the valley were steep and rugged, the erosion rapid. So obviously the dinosaurs moved through a valley leaving footprints in the soft sediments of those times. Subsequently the sand hardened to sandstone, the mud to shale. When geological history is expressed in terms of eras and periods, we gain an impression of what the conditions were at that time.

Relating the past to significant events is not especially unique. In geology, where earth history is involved, the big events used to measure time are the episodes of mountain building. Of course, mountains are not built abruptly; the change takes time.

The time before the Appalachians were built is known as the Paleozoic Era. *Paleo-* is a term that comes from the Greek and means "ancient." Likewise, *zoic* means "life," as in zoology. Thus Paleozoic means "ancient life."

The Rocky Mountains are younger than the Appalachians. The time during which the Rockies were elevated marks another division of time. The long interval from after the Appalachians were built until the Rocky Mountains were uplifted is termed the Mesozoic Era. *Meso-* means "middle," so that Mesozoic indicates "middle life," when living things were more highly developed than during the Paleozoic Era.

In the Far West most of the significant geological events have occurred since the Rocky Mountains were uplifted, during the Cenozoic Era. In this case, *ceno-* indicates common or recent. Even so, the Cenozoic comprises a long span of time with many changes in living creatures and in the land itself. The Cascade Range, for example, developed during the Cenozoic Era, as did common farm animals. Even human beings evolved during the long Cenozoic Era.

According to rough modern estimates, the Appalachian Mountains were uplifted about 200 million years ago. The Rocky Mountains developed about 70 million years ago. The Cascade Mountains were elevated about a million years ago and are still being uplifted. Older dates are even more indefinite, the numbers less significant than the relationships to other events at that time.

Because the eras of Earth's history are so long, they are further divided into periods. The first and oldest period of the Paleozoic Era, long before the Appalachians were built, was the Cambrian, which began about 600 million years ago. Once it was thought that no living things existed before the Cambrian Period. In a sense that is still true, because no conspicuous fossils can be found in rocks that predate the Cambrian. However, colonies of fossilized algae have been found in Precambrian rocks. Worm holes in rocks of that age provide further evidence of simple life forms before the Cambrian period. Deposits of carbon, thought to be the remains of living things, also have been found—but without bones or shells to make them readily identifiable.

Very old rocks are ordinarily termed Precambrian formations. The Precambrian marks a very long span of time—about four billion years—as compared with the half billion years from the beginning of the Cambrian to the present. The broad interior of Canada, the Canadian Shield, consists of Precambrian rocks, some as much as 2½ billion years old. The Adirondacks in upstate New York are Precambrian, and so are the rocks at the western end of Lake Superior, where Duluth is located. In New York City, the gnarled rocks (Fordham gneiss) of the Bronx are Precambrian, too.

During the Devonian Period, which is near the middle of the Paleozoic Era, about 350 million years ago, primitive fish existed in the oceans, which comprised a much greater area than they do now. Seashells are common in the rocks of today's upper New York State, because the land of the Devonian Period was under water. The shells are found in rocks formed from sediment washed off mountains uplifted in what is now New England. Also found in the sediments of what was then an inland sea are sharks' teeth, which shows that those "boneless fish" already existed in Devonian times. The granite of the White Mountains in New Hampshire was uplifted and hardened at this time; and sands washed off the Acadian Mountains to form the Catskills at the mouth of a stream that no longer exists. Some primitive tree fossils at Gilboa in the Catskills were alive on the foothills of mountains at the edge of the inland sea. Hardened sediments of Devonian age also are found as rocks in the Genesse Gorge and in the gorge at Niagara Falls.

The next two periods, the Mississippian and the Pennsylvanian, are named after significant formations in the United States. In Europe these two periods together are known as the Carboniferous. Swampy lowlands at that time—about 300 million years ago—were common in many areas, including the Appalachian region and the Midwest, where today we find deposits of coal. Primitive forests grew in those swamps. When the vegetation died and fell into the shallow water, the plant materials only partially decayed. Beneath the water there was a shortage of the oxygen needed to promote the decay in which carbon dioxide is formed. The carbon remained in the swamps and was altered to become coal. In Pennsylvania, where later mountain-building pressures were intense, the carbon was hardened as anthracite coal.

During the Mississippian Period, much of what is the Midwest today was under water. Lime precipitated from the water, forming thick deposits that now are limestone. In Kentucky the Mammoth Caves developed in that thick mass of limestone. During these times limestone was also formed in Oklahoma, Indiana, and other states of the interior. The limestone indicates that much of the interior throughout this portion of the Paleozoic Era was a lowland with lime settling out of water. As the land began to rise a bit, the seas retreated and swamplands developed in shallow water. From the partial decay of vegetation in the swamps have come coal fields.

As the regional uplifts continued, the lowlands in the Southwest were compressed, and mountain ranges were formed across Oklahoma. The remains of those mountains are the Arbuckle Upland, the Wichita Mountains, and the Amarillo Mountains of the Texas Panhandle. Later, when the Rocky Mountains were uplifted, the remains of the old Amarillo Mountains were entirely buried under sediments washed off the Rockies, so that the former mountains are no longer visible at the surface. Late in the Paleozoic Era, mountain building resumed in the Southwest with the uplift of the Ouachita Mountains as an eastward extension of the Wichita-Arbuckle Range. Concurrently, the Appalachians began to develop in the East, with a southwestern extension that suggests the Ouachita uplift was somehow related.

The Acadian Mountains in New England were followed by the formation of the more extensive Appalachian Range, which serves to mark the
end of the Paleozoic Era.

Marking time by the mountains gives us a strong frame of reference on
which to build a coherent picture of the past. In terms of eras and periods,
we can see how conditions at any one time were interrelated and how
new conditions developed out of former ones—a process that continues
even today.

3

UPLIFT OF THE ROCKY MOUNTAINS AND THE SOUTHWEST

Long ago, before the Rocky Mountains were uplifted, the land was depressed and covered by seawater. The depression extended northward across the span of the western United States and Canada into the Arctic. Southward the flooded area included much of Mexico and Central America. Gradually the pressures that depressed the area shifted and caused the land to rise somewhat, so that large areas became shallow swamplands. The vegetation that flourished in those swamps eventually formed deep beds of carbon that later became the coal now mined in Alberta, Wyoming, and elsewhere in the Rocky Mountains.

Apparently, the Rocky Mountains were uplifted by deep-seated pressures much as the mountains of Alaska are being elevated today. Pressures from the west not only lifted the land but also caused massive rock formations to fold as they were shoved upward. In some places the rocks were broken and pushed eastward, forming thrust faults. One great thrust fault is prominent in Glacier National Park, Montana, where the massive Lewis Overthrust has been forced out over younger land, at the start of the Great Plains. The huge mass of a mountain 50 miles wide was gradually shoved toward the east more than 15 miles.

In Utah, near Salt Lake City, the Wasatch Mountain Range rises abruptly, forming a prominent wall facing the lowland in which the Great Salt Lake is located, along with such cities as Ogden and Salt Lake City. Under the great pressures of mountain building, solid bedrock was broken, forming what is known as a normal fault, where one side of the break slides downward in relation to the other. The normal fault was so named because of the belief of early geologists that this was the primary, typical kind of fault. In contrast, the San Andreas Fault in California is termed a *transverse fault,* because the movement is predominantly sidewise, or horizontal.

Another spectacular example of a normal, or vertical, fault is in the Teton Mountain Range a short way south of Yellowstone Park. Granitoid rocks there have been lifted on one side of a major fault, forming a wall of mountains facing east. Erosion has cut into the uplifted side of the fault, shaping it into a range of mountain peaks high and rugged, the highest peak being Grand Teton—at 13,800 feet, one of the tallest mountain peaks in the contiguous United States.

A short distance south of the Wyoming border in Utah are the Uinta Mountains. The pressured land there has bulged upward in what geologists call an anticline. Erosion has cut into the uplifted surface to form a broad range of mountains.

The wide Colorado Plateau is located in the heart of the Rocky Mountains, extending across Colorado into Utah and southward through much of Arizona and New Mexico. The distinctive feature of the plateau is land that has been uplifted more than two miles, yet much of it remains a rather flat surface. Layers of now-elevated sediment are still horizontal in the midst of rugged mountains. The Colorado River has cut into this surface, forming the Grand Canyon and revealing uniform strata, one layer upon another, with older, massive rocks at the bottom of the canyon.

As shown here, the Rocky Mountains are high and truly massive. This pass is almost 2½ miles high. Even as the mountains are uplifted, erosion is cutting into them, as can be seen to the right of the sign.

Batholiths

On the Great Plains, the Front Range of the Rocky Mountains can be seen as a wall of mountains, standing high above Denver. Though located on the High Plains, Denver is truly a "mile high city." From Denver the Great Plains slope eastward to lower levels. In the Front Range above Denver are some of the highest mountains of the southern Rockies, including Long's Peak, which stands well above 14,000 feet—close to three miles high. During the building of the Rocky Mountains, massive granitoid rocks rose from the depths in what geologists call batholiths. The mountains near Denver are a fine example. As massive rock from the depths was gradually elevated, less resistant rocks above were worn away, leaving the granite standing bare in prominences such as Long's Peak and rounded domes such as Bald Mountain. Rocky Mountain National Park is located in this area, and the continental divide bisects the park.

Similar rock masses are prominent throughout the Rocky Mountains from Idaho northward along the west coast of Canada, where the Rockies and Coast Ranges merge as one great range running all the way into Alaska. Further great batholiths are prominent in the Sierra Nevada, visible as broad prominences at Yosemite, Sequoia, and King's Canyon national parks.

Yellowstone Park is noted for its geysers, mud pots, and hot springs. All of these are heated by hot subterranean rocks. In the case of mud pots, heated groundwater bubbles up through the muddy surface. As steam pressure mounts, the mud and steam are ejected in what is loosely termed a mud volcano. The ejections tend to build up small cones of mud, which resemble tiny volcanoes. Spectacular geysers are created when surface water seeps into openings in the rocks and is heated by the rocks below. If the opening from above is small, so that surface water fills the opening, the heated water below becomes steam. When the steam pressure is great enough to eject the column of water confining it, the geyser erupts.

These mud pots and geysers indicate that the rocks just below the surface are hot, which suggests that a degree of volcanic activity persists, but to a degree insufficient to cause an eruption. Apparently, recent extensive lava flows have occurred there. Yellowstone Park is located on a comparatively flat surface and is considered a plateau, though close examination reveals that a great volcano once erupted there. After the eruption the volcano collapsed, and the crater and caldera became filled with sediment, forming the flat surface of a plateau; only remnants of the former volcano remain as an indistinct rim. So the geysers and hot springs provide evidence that the subterranean disturbances have not completely ceased.

Moreover, the Yellowstone area is contiguous with the lava fields of Idaho, including those that constitute the Craters of the Moon National Monument. The lava fields of Idaho extend north and south as a wide border along the western side of the Rocky Mountains. In Alaska, the Alaska Range from Mount McKinley to the Aleutian Islands and beyond likewise is bordered by volcanoes and lava flows. The eruptions there are close to the source of pressure from the advancing ocean bed. It seems that the mountain building and lava flows of Alaska demonstrate how the

With the elevation of the Rocky Mountains there were lava flows over wide areas along the western border of the uplifted mountains. Broad scenes such as this in eastern Washington, extending from the Canadian border through Oregon into Utah and Nevada, are typical of the region.

Rocky Mountains and adjoining lava fields were built over a period of more than 70 million years. The uplift of the Rocky Mountains and the great lava flows were somewhat more extensive than the similar upheavals in Alaska; however, the mountain building in Alaska is continuing. And if it persists for millions of years, as did the Rocky Mountain Revolution, the Alaska Range could become far more extensive than it is today. For now, the upheavals in Alaska provide a demonstration of the way mountain ranges are built.

The Great Basin and the Sierra Nevada

Following the uplift of the Rocky Mountains and the building of the adjoining lava fields, the region of most active mountain building has gradually shifted westward as the continent continues to drift in that direction. With the westward movement has come the building of new mountains, the Cascades, Sierra Nevada, and Coast Ranges.

In Utah and Nevada the westward shift of mountain-building pressures has caused the hardened rocks of the lava fields to bulge and break into segments. Those segments have been elevated on one side to form ridges, with the opposite sides becoming depressed to form basins between the ridges. The result has been the formation of parallel basins and ranges in much of Utah and Nevada.

Currently in California, friction from northward movement of the ocean bed west of the San Andreas Fault seems to be dragging with it a broad region of southern California and Nevada, stretching and depressing the Great Basin, the region of basins and ranges west of the southern Rockies. The depressed basin has no outlet to the sea; streams end there as inland bodies of water. Since the leeward side of mountain ranges is a dry area, evaporation is rapid. Ordinarily evaporation is about as rapid as the inflow of water from streams, maintaining an equilibrium, but whatever minerals are washed into the lakes are left behind as the water evaporates.

Great Salt Lake, for example, becomes increasingly salty as streams bring in more and more minerals from the regions drained. There was a time during the Ice Age when precipitation was more abundant than it is today. Consequently, the level of the lake was much higher than now, high enough that an outlet was found to the north through Idaho and into the Snake River. While the lake was at that higher level, waves on the surface cut into the mountainside, the west wall of the Wasatch Range, developing a notch, a benchmark for the level of the lake. As the outlet in Idaho was lowered by erosion, the water level in the lake was lowered too. A series of level lines can be seen on the wall where the Wasatch Range was uplifted along a great fault line. The lines are notches worn by waves on the surface of the lake, and they reveal the heights of the lake at various stages in the past. With the lake now far below the former outlet, the height of the water in Great Salt Lake remains low, except for variations in the seasonal rainfall.

The Great Basin is bordered on the west by the Sierra Nevada. Geologists call the Sierra "block mountains," likening them to a solid block that has been tipped up on its edge, forming an abrupt wall on the eastern side with a gradual slope to the west. The uplifted block is mostly a solid mass of granite. Mount Whitney, the highest peak in the contiguous United States, stands on that elevated eastern edge.

Prevailing westerly winds off the ocean to the west are cooled as they rise, much as in the Cascades farther north. Although the precipitation at this latitude is not as great, it has been sufficient in the past to produce snow at high elevations. The snow was compacted, forming glaciers, and the glaciers cut into the surface to form rounded valleys and jagged mountain peaks. A few such glaciers remain.

Descending currents of air on the abrupt eastern face of the Sierra have an even more pronounced effect than that of the Cascades, so that the Owens Valley, a lowland bordering the Sierras on the east, is quite dry. The broad Mojave Desert and arid Death Valley National Monument are both in the rain shadow of the Sierras, demonstrating the effect of mountains on rainfall.

Along the major faults where the Sierra have been uplifted, weathering has moved the rocky bluff back somewhat from where the faults occur. At ground level the broken rocks along the actual fault also have been subjected to accelerated erosion. The result is a depression, a ravine where the fault occurred. So today, in the otherwise dry Owens Valley, a small stream from the north flows in the ravine along the face of the uplifted bluff.

Due east of San Francisco in the uplifted Sierra Nevada, a branch road from Mammoth Lakes leads to a prominent lava flow known as the Devil's Postpile, a national monument. As the dark basaltic lava cooled, it formed six-sided columns, a huge stack of tall posts standing in a bunch, the shape indicative of columnar jointing, which is typical of basaltic lava. Another site of volcanic activity is found in the nearby and aptly named Mammoth

A normal fault in the Inyo National Forest of the Sierra Nevada of California, south of Mount Whitney, the highest peak, and west of Death Valley, the lowest point, in the region. Uplift of the land has resulted in the fault shown here.

Lakes. Located near the southern rim of what was once a huge volcano, it is what geologists call a caldera. Like Crater Lake in Oregon, it is a volcanic mountain that exploded then collapsed long ago, leaving an oblong depression 10 miles wide and twice as long, surrounded by a ring of hills. The hills mark the base of the former volcano, somewhat compressed between two mountain ranges, the Sierra and the White Mountains of Nevada. Since the volcano was destroyed in a violent eruption, periodic disturbances have built a line of small volcanic craters along the major fault line, running from the northernmost, Mono Lake, into the caldera of the former great volcano.

Off and on in recent years there have been further disturbances in the vicinity, indicating that mountain building is continuing. Major earthquakes indicate that the Sierra Nevada is still rising. The recent disturbances suggest that molten rock—magma—may be rising toward the surface. So far, there has been no eruption, though a broad region within the old caldera has bulged upward as much as 10 inches. Such bulges can be significant. A bulge on the north slope of Mount Saint Helens accompanied by tremors preceded the violent eruption there in 1980. Since that eruption, continuing activity within the hollow shell of the mountain is building an interior dome, as is typical of volcanic mountains such as Vesuvius in Italy. The disturbances at Mammoth Lakes may presage further eruptions there, too.

Nearby, but higher in the Sierras, is Yosemite National Park and its famed Yosemite Valley, Half Dome, Yosemite Falls, and other featured

The Devil's Postpile, once-molten rock that rose along the fault line of the Owens Valley, where the Sierra Nevada were uplifted. Cooling caused the basaltic rock to shrink and form columns that resemble posts.

Yosemite Valley in the Sierra Nevada. Half Dome, at the center of the picture, is a massive granite uplift, typical of the Sierra Nevada. The meadow was once a glacial lake.

sights. East of Fresno, California, is Kings Canyon National Park, with Sequoia National Park just beyond. These large parks cover much of the western slope of the Sierra Nevada, and all reveal the exposed granite domes of which the mountain ranges are made.

In southern California, though the San Andreas Fault is predominant, there are other significant fractures in the bedrock, some of which have produced mountains. The San Bernardino Mountains just east of Los Angeles, for example, have been uplifted along a fault more or less parallel to the San Andreas Fault where it bends inland toward the Salton Sea and the Gulf of California.

Here in Kings Canyon National Park in the Sierra Nevada, boulders tumble down from the heights of a granite dome and, jostling together in a stream, become rounded, illustrating how all boulders and smaller stones are formed.

Farther north in California, at Mendocino, is a major transverse fault, so called because it extends from west to east, rather than north and south as do most faults in the region. The Mendocino Fault runs eastward to form the northern end of the Sierra Nevada. Farther west near the coast are the Klamath Mountains, on the north side of the same fault line. The Klamath Mountains are remarkably similar to the Sierra Nevada. It seems as though transverse movements along the fault have separated what originally was a continuing range of mountains. Concurrent with that disturbance along the transverse fault, and over an immense period of time, eruptions of lava built the wide lava fields at the northern end of the Sierra Nevada. Mount Shasta, at the western edge of those lava fields and just north of the transverse fault, is evidently another result of the disturbance along that fault. Shasta has been active in the comparatively recent past, and so have some portions of the lava fields. Likewise, earthquakes have accompanied further elevation of the Sierra Nevada; so in terms of geological time, mountain building there seems to be continuing.

Scenic Wonders of the Southwest

From the shores of California to the Grand Canyon and beyond are many picturesque scenes, providing evidence of forces that shape the Earth. From Redwood National Park, near the Oregon border, southward along the coast to Muir Woods National Monument, located close to San Francisco Bay, the majestic redwoods of the California coast are certainly impressive. Yet the redwoods are puny in comparison to the immense forces that shaped the Klamath Mountains in that area and produced the geysers near Cloverdale. Also of special interest is the Point Reyes National Seashore where the great San Andreas Fault extends out to sea. On the coast just north of San Francisco, this fault line is readily identified by a narrow, straight-line bay, a depression along the geological fault separating Point Reyes from the mainland. From the north end of the Golden Gate Bridge, a highway leads out along the coast to the Muir Woods and Point Reyes just beyond.

Once a network of merging river valleys, like Puget Sound, San Francisco Bay was produced by the downfolding and faulting of a depressed area, which includes San Pablo Bay to the north, the Santa Clara Valley southward to the Bay of Monterey, and the valley from which the Salinas River empties into the bay at Monterey. Farther inland, even the Great Central Valley of California was folded downward between the Sierra Nevada and Coast Ranges by pressures derived from the westward drift of the continent.

South of Salinas is the Pinnacles National Monument, with its rocky spires and domes as the only remaining evidence of a volcano long since inactive. Along the coast south of Monterey and the scenic Big Sur sit many flat terraces, indicating that the land has risen from sea level. As waves continue to cut into the shore, forming flat surfaces at water level, these too, with further uplift of the land, will become terraces above sea level. If, as at Monterey and Santa Cruz, some rock formations are hard and resistant to the waves, those rocks may be left standing after the surrounding land has been cut back, forming the sea stacks, arches, and other prominences seen out of surrounding water close to shore. Finer particles of rock, pulverized by the waves, become beach sand.

Long ago in the depressed Los Angeles Basin, when petroleum seeped to the surface, the lighter elements evaporated, leaving only sticky tar and forming what is today known as the La Brea Tar Pits. During the Ice Age, when animals blundered into the tar and became mired down, predators came to attack but also ended up sinking into the congealed tar. As a result, the remains of a great variety of Ice Age animals have been found in the tar, including mastodons, wooly mammoths, saber-toothed tigers, camels, tapirs, giant ground sloths, and other such extinct animals. The tar pits are located on Wilshire Boulevard in Hancock Park, Los Angeles. Restorations of the remains can be seen at the county museum there.

Moving South, in San Diego at Point Loma there is further evidence that the Pacific Coast is rising, for the uplifted shore there has been shaped by the impact of ocean waves, forming what is known as Sunset Cliffs. San Diego is located on the ocean side of California's Coastal Mountain Range, which extends southward to the Mexican border and beyond as the peninsular backbone of Baja (Lower) California. The mountain range separates balmy San Diego from a Desert State Park, creating a remarkable climatic difference and proving once again that mountains have great influence on the weather. East of the mountains and beyond the park is the lowland Imperial Valley, essentially an extension of the submerged Gulf of California. Both are products of the San Andreas Fault, which runs through the Imperial Valley southward into the Gulf of California and northward along the east side of the Salton Sea, a body of water 235 feet below sea level. Sediment washed into the Imperial Valley by the Colorado River, when irrigated by water from the river, has converted the desert to a region of highly productive truck gardens, El Centro being the marketing center.

Crossing the Laguna Mountains out of San Diego into the Imperial Valley, the highway descends diagonally along a sheer bluff, a fault line along which the coastal mountains were elevated while the Imperial Valley was being depressed. The San Andreas is the major fault, but the region is broken with numerous faults, elevating mountains from Santa Barbara to San Bernardino. Joshua trees, now protected in the national monument of that name, are related to the smaller, more common yucca plant. The monument is located in the southern portion of the Mojave Desert, where Joshua trees as much as 40 feet high are dwarfed by towering "castles" of weathered granite, outliers of the San Bernardino Mountains, which have been uplifted by faulting. Still farther north, beyond the Mojave Desert is Death Valley, a national monument. The inland area is consistently dry due to the coastal mountains.

Continuing eastward into the mountains at Flagstaff, we enter a region of towering pines, home to Sunset Crater, a national monument. Although the volcano last erupted more than 900 years ago, the lava flow remains fresh in the dry air of the region. The tall cinder cone seems to glow in the light of the setting sun, giving the peak its name. Adjoining Sunset Crater on the north is the Wupatki National Monument, a primitive Indian settlement with the ruins of buildings constructed of stone, and a circular amphitheater, believed to have been designed as a sports arena for a game similar to a ball game played in ancient Mexico.

East of Flagstaff, beyond Winslow and Holbrook, is the Petrified Forest National Park. The park has an abundance of logs, now preserved as hard rock. These logs were once trees that were uprooted in floods and washed into an eddy during the time when this region was a lowland. Minerals soaked into the tree trunks as the wood decayed, replacing the wood bit by bit with colorful quartz yet preserving the outlines of the wood. To the north, across the highway, is the Painted Desert, featuring the same colorful minerals as those of the Petrified Forest. The Painted Desert is a vast area, now largely a Hopi Indian Reservation.

Also east of Flagstaff, but closer to the city, is Walnut Canyon, a national monument containing prehistoric Indian dwellings in the canyon walls, visible from the visitor's center at the canyon rim.

The most impressive landform of all, the Grand Canyon, is not far north of Flagstaff. Since the elevation of the Colorado Plateau, the Colorado River has cut a deep and extensive canyon in the sediments deposited there while the region was a lowland. The Grand Canyon is fascinating because of its sheer size, yet it is far more than a spectacle, for it demonstrates what unchecked erosion can do to the land. Even more profound is what it reveals of Earth's history.

The layers of rock exposed one upon another, like the pages of a history book, provide a record of the changes that have occurred throughout the ages. At the bottom of the canyon are the oldest, Precambrian rocks. The ones above are succeedingly younger. Geologists speak of this as *superposition,* when the strata of sedimentary rocks provide a record of geological history. But more than that, fossils in the rocks give us a record of the plants and animals that existed during each age. At the bottom, in the Precambrian rocks, are found only fossils of very simple, scarcely recognizable forms. At higher levels, more complex, well-developed fossils are found. The changes appear gradual, with upper-level fossils similar to those just below, indicating that the more advanced forms apparently developed from the more simple ones found at lower levels. Or to generalize, it is apparent that higher forms of plants and animals have evolved from the simpler ones below. Yet some simple plants, such as algae, have survived without much change.

The rocks of the Grand Canyon represent an immense period of time and many changes, our most complete record of early geological and biological changes. But the Grand Canyon does not stand alone. Findings in other locations have correlated and extended the record of past ages.

South of the Great Basin in Utah are a number of national parks and monuments featuring spectacular scenes shaped by erosion of the Colorado Plateau: Bryce, Zion, Canyonlands, Arches, and Capitol Reef national parks. Less extensive are the Cedar Breaks, Natural Bridge, Rainbow Bridge, and Timpanogos Cave national monuments. In each of these, less resistant sandstone and other sedimentary rocks, deposited when the region was a lowland, have been removed by erosion, with what remains forming spectacular rugged peaks. The flat surface of the plateau stands in plain sight at a higher level, revealing the surface as it was before erosion cut into it. Minerals of red, yellow, and other colors in the sediments help to color the scenes. Where a stratum of hard rock remains standing after weak sediment below has been cut away, a natural bridge is formed, one of the more unusual geological rock formations. At Timpanogos Cave, limestone caverns are featured. Throughout the region, spectacular erosion has revealed what lies below the great plateau and suggests what happened there in ages past. In some locations we find lavas that erupted while the plateau was being uplifted.

The scenes in Zion National Park are especially noteworthy. The rocks of Zion, like those of the Grand Canyon, reveal the Paleozoic history of changes in the Earth and life upon it. But Zion serves to extend the account into more recent times. Along with the neighboring Bryce Canyon National Park, Mesozoic and early Cenozoic (Tertiary) rocks contain the bones of Mesozoic dinosaurs and even more recent fossils that show the continuing development of life on Earth, along with changes in the climate and the landscape itself. Erosion has been more severe in the Grand

In Bryce Canyon National Park erosion of the uplifted Colorado Plateau has produced spectacular scenery. The original surface is visible at the top of the picture. In this dry region, much of the erosion is due to wind-blown sand.

Canyon region, so that more recent rocks and fossils, being at the top, are completely removed, whereas they remain in the Bryce and Zion areas.

At Zion, there is a massive rock formation known as the Great White Throne, also a rock organ for the temple, a rock Tower of the Virgin, and a rock Altar of Sacrifices—all carved by nature. At Cedar City, a short way north, is Cedar Breaks National Monument, featuring an "amphitheater" of eroded sandstone and limestone in striking colors. This monument could be considered an adjunct of nearby Bryce, for the two are carved from the same geological formations of sedimentary rocks, which in ages past were sediments washed into the lowland.

Bryce Canyon National Park is just about the ultimate erosional spectacle, with innumerable spires and a huge arch that resembles a bridge. Another especially noteworthy scenic area is Arches National Park, located near the Colorado border. Eighty-one natural arches span the park. Landscape Arch is said to be the longest natural bridge in the world.

Across the state line in Colorado is the Mesa Verde National Park, said to contain the finest prehistoric Indian cliff dwellings in this country. The green tableland of Mesa Verde is cut with numerous canyons. Clusters of complex dwellings can be seen in caves and in the walls of canyons.

Farther south in New Mexico, beyond the town of Shiprock, is the "Shiprock" itself. According to a Navajo myth, when the tribe was attacked by Utes, the besieged tribe took refuge on the prominence, which promptly sprouted wings and flew the Navajos to safety. We now know that Shiprock is a volcanic neck, the center of a volcano that remained after the surrounding mountain had been removed by erosion.

4

UPLIFT OF THE APPALACHIANS

The uplift of the Appalachians marks a transition in geological time, the end of the Paleozoic Era, during which readily discernible life forms developed.

Throughout the Paleozoic, a great depression grew in the Appalachian region. The depression extended south to north, from what is now the Gulf of Mexico through Canada and beyond what now is Newfoundland. That lowland was eventually covered by marine waters and persisted through the Paleozoic until eventually the Appalachians were uplifted from out of the depression. The Rocky Mountains, which were to come later, were also built where a depressed seaway had existed, and share certain similarities.

For a long time it was clear to geologists that pressures from the ocean gradually elevated the mountains and closed the eastern seaway, but the

Across Lake Champlain, near Burlington, Vermont, is a major fault where dolomite limestone has been thrust out over a much darker calcareous shale, made from clay and lime. This fault occurred as the Appalachians were being uplifted.

source of these pressures was unknown. Thrust faults are still prominent throughout the region, and a good example is the thrust fault near Burlington, Vermont. From south of the city it is easy to see how a cliff of hard dolomite limestone has been shoved out over darker layers of shale. The fault is quite prominent where exposed, but it actually extends deep into the earth far northward into Canada. The Green Mountains of Vermont were shoved inland along this fault and now stand as a wall above the lowland of Lake Champlain.

Other such thrust faults are readily visible in West Virginia, where hard sandstone has been forced up over less rigid beds of coal. Another prominent example is found farther south in the Pine Mountains near the

In western Virginia, near Richlands, pressures from the east caused layered rock, or strata, to fold as shown here. The mountains here are often spoken of as the "Folded Appalachians."

The solid rocks of New England are twisted and complex, due to pressures experienced in the mantle during mountain-building episodes.

Cumberland Gap and the Kentucky-Tennessee border. There hard sand-stone and conglomerate (solid rock of sand and stones) have been shoved upward to form the Cumberland Mountains. These and numerous other thrust faults indicate that pressures from the coast compressed the sedi-ments that had accumulated in the depression and forced them upward to form the lofty Appalachian Mountain Range.

In many cases the rocks under pressure during faulting were bent instead of broken, forming folds, much like the pages of a book when pressure is applied to the sides. In the Appalachians, pressures from the direction of the ocean forced huge folds into tall mountains. Long since, these mountains have been worn away, leaving only the stumps of those mountains, not unlike the stumps of trees. These stumps are too extensive to be seen in a single view, but the rocks under pressure have crumpled to show smaller folds seen in roadside rock banks.

As has been noted, the Cascade Mountains were built largely of lava flows, and the volcanic eruptions there continue today. The volcanoes of the Appalachians are gone now, worn away in ages past, but we can see where eruptions once occurred. To reach the surface as lava, molten rock has to be forced up from below. Although the volcanic peaks are gone, we can see where molten rock squeezed through the stumps of the former mountains. Near Boston, Massachusetts, in rocks along the shore there are many such intrusions, visible as dark basalt contrasting with the lighter granitelike rocks that were the base of the mountains. In the Appalachians today there is much evidence of how these mountains were formed. Thrust faults show the results of pressures from the east that broke the rocks and shoved them upward. The immense pressures caused the rocks in many cases to buckle and fold as they were forced upward. Often the mountains are spoken of as the "Folded Appalachians," because such buckling was so common. As in the West today, volcanic eruptions were frequent as the Appalachians were being uplifted. Thrust faults, folding, and abundant evidence of volcanoes and lava flows reveal the forces behind the formation of the Appalachians.

Here molten dark basalt was forced up through joints in the lighter colored granite as the mountains were being uplifted. If the basalt reached the surface, it would have been as lava, but the surface here at Boston has been worn away.

Giant conglomerate near Boston. The stones became rounded in a swift mountain stream that flowed out of mountains formerly to the east of our East Coast, now the west side of Africa. The boulders are in a solid mass of rock.

Continental Drift and the Pressures of Mountain Building

In Massachusetts on the outskirts of Boston, just south of the city, is a mass of giant conglomerate. Conglomerate is solid rock made up largely of sand and rounded stones cemented together by minerals from water in the bed of a former stream. Conglomerate may be likened to concrete, in which sand and gravel have become a solid mass held together with a "glue" made largely from limestone. Conglomerate once was known as "pudding stone," because of a superficial resemblance to pudding with raisins in it. Rounded stones ordinarily are found only in swift streams where broken rocks tumble over each other and become worn, and well rounded in the fast-flowing water. Many of the stones in the giant conglomerate are very large. Such boulders are found only in steep mountains where streams are especially swift. Close to the shore of Massachusetts Bay and the Atlantic Ocean, though there is no stream at all today, the boulders indicate that there must have been a swift mountain stream there some time in the distant past. Moreover, it is evident the stream flowed westward, because the conglomerate stones become smaller farther west, as do the stones in streams that flow down out of mountains into a lowland, losing their force. So it seems this former stream came down out of mountains farther

Conglomerate rock in Boston a bit farther inland than the giant conglomerate on page 57. The smaller stones indicate the stream was flowing westward out of mountains to lower ground. Farther inland the stones decreased in size as the current slowed, aiding erosion.

east, even though there are no mountains farther east—nothing but Massachusetts Bay and the Atlantic Ocean.

Geologists and oceanographers in recent years have found an explanation for this apparent mystery—*plate tectonics,* more commonly known as continental drift. This theory states that continents are not completely immobile, in fixed positions, as they seem to be. Instead they gradualy drift about on the surface of the Earth. The movement is not perceptible in a human lifetime but only over vast periods of time. About a million years ago, before there was an Atlantic Ocean, the continent of Africa pressed tightly against what is now our east coast. Like two heavy trucks crashing head-on (but in slow motion), the continents pressed against each other. Where the impact occurred, the land crumpled, causing the folding of rocks and mountain building, with molten rock welling up from below. Unlike a collision of trucks, the pressures on our east coast were almost imperceptible. Not only were the Appalachians elevated, but so were the Atlas Mountains of Northwest Africa. Now Africa is drifting in another direction, with the Atlantic Ocean filling the void. Today Africa is pressing northward against Europe, uplifting the Alps and causing volcanoes to erupt, as they have repeatedly in Italy at Vesuvius and Etna.

Conglomerate is a common rock throughout the Boston Basin, especially in the Roxbury section of the city; hence the formation is termed *Roxbury conglomerate.* In the Boston Basin the rounded stones of the conglomerate are large but not as large as those in the giant conglomerate found closer to the shore. Apparently, still finer sediments of sand were washed farther west, but the uplift and erosion of the Appalachians have removed the evidence. Yet it is plainly evident that the ancient stream flowed west out of mountains in the east, the Atlas Mountains of Africa. One bit of far-out speculation assumes the westward-flowing stream carried sand and mud directly across what is now Massachusetts. There at the western border of the state the Taconic Mountains consist of what was once a vast amount of such sediments, now consolidated as solid rock.

Plate tectonics and the drifting of continents explain the source of pressures that built the Appalachians. The situation was comparable to what is happening in Alaska today, with the northward pressure of the Pacific Ocean bed elevating the Alaskan Range and causing numerous volcanic eruptions. Likewise, the Himalayas, currently the most massive of all mountains, are attributed to the northward drift of India, now pressing against Asia. In America the Roxbury conglomerate is good evidence, but by no means the only instance, of eastern streams that once flowed westward into what is now the United States. Before the plate tectonics concept was developed, geologists found it difficult to explain how abundant sediments from the east washed into the great Appalachian depression and beyond to form what are now the Appalachian plateaus. The best explanation available assumed there were once mountains along what is now our east coast, mountains that since have been completely destroyed by erosion. All that remained of those mountains were the hard rocks of their base, still evident beneath the coastal sands, together with those of the Piedmont. In a way, that explanation was to some extent true, for it has become apparent that those hard rocks along our shore were at the base of mountains, but mountains that now are in Northeast Africa.

Volcanoes and Lava in the Appalachians

Just as the damage at Mount Saint Helens shows what happened there a few years ago, the rocks of the Appalachians reveal what happened much farther back in the past. When studied, these rocks provide vivid accounts of volcanoes and earthquakes, of mountains that have come and gone.

Once-molten rock from deep within the earth is conspicuous throughout the Connecticut Valley, extending into Massachusetts and southward into New Jersey in what may have been a continuous lowland now interrupted by Long Island Sound. When the Appalachians were built, the Connecticut Valley was depressed between two tall mountains. As inevitably happens, snow and rain washed much sand and clay into the valley below. That sand eventually formed sandstone and the clay, shale. Iron in the sediments oxidized, giving both the sandstone and shale a reddish color. With continuing crustal disturbances, lava oozed out from below to spread across the valley in broad sheets, something like the lava fields of the West. After the lava beds had cooled and hardened, further crustal disturbances broke the basaltic sheets of rock and tipped them up, one broken edge higher than the other, not unlike what happened to the lava fields of Utah and Nevada at a much later date. As with those fields, the uplifted edges of hard rock in the Connecticut Valley formed ridges with gentle slopes on one side, steep cliffs on the other where the fault occurred. There are many such ridges in the valley, termed "trap" ridges locally. The Hanging Hills at Meriden, Connecticut, are one prominent example; Mount Tom in the Holyoke Range of Massachusetts is another; West Rock at New Haven is another basaltic prominence. Just north is Mount Carmel, a low ridge of black rock also known as the "Sleeping Giant," because it has the appearance of a large man lying on his back. In the valley there were three successive sheets of lava. In some cases the rock is too coarse-grained to be a true basalt, but nevertheless falls under the classification of trap ridges. Where the rock is coarse-grained, the large crystals indicate the molten rock cooled slowly, allowing time for the crystals to grow before the rock hardened. Ordinarily the large crystals indicate that the rock hardened below the surface, slowing its cooling. Or the molten rock could have been lava on the surface, subsequently covered by sediment washed down on top of it following disturbances in the mountains, allowing it to cool slowly with time for crystals to grow. Variation in the size of crystals may indicate that some of the lava was covered by more of the sediment, hence cooling more slowly than the lava in other locations.

In New Jersey, the Watchung Mountains are trap ridges like those of the Connecticut Valley with similar red sandstone between the ridges. Just across the Hudson River from New York City are the Palisades. The rock of the Palisades is basaltic, a molten mass that rose from the earth's depths as the mountains were being uplifted. The large crystals here indicate that the rock was not a lava but spread horizontally as a sill beneath overlying rocks. The molten mass, thus covered, cooled slowly, allowing time for large crystals to form. As the molten mass cooled, it shrank a bit and became broken with joints. With the rock cover now removed by erosion, the vertical joints give the mass of rock on the riverbank an appearance similar to the upright posts of a stockade. In colonial times a fence of vertical posts serving to protect a fort or a village was known as a palisade, hence the name.

Along the rocky shores of New England the granitelike rocks from the base of the old mountains in numerous instances contain broad lines of a darker rock where lava emerged. Such volcanic intrusions are termed *dikes,* for where the intrusions occur in soft rocks near the surface, the less resistant rock is commonly worn away, leaving the intrusion standing alone, vertically, as a wall of hard rock, which may look like a flood wall, or dike. The term is now applied to all vertical intrusions. Where the molten rock has been forced out horizontally into other rocks below the surface, the formation is known as a *sill,* like a window sill, the horizontal portion at the base of a window. The Palisades along the Hudson River were formed as a sill, though it is now exposed on the surface.

In suburban Newton, Massachusetts, on Lowell Street, just north of Commonwealth Avenue beyond the city limits of Boston, a school has been built in an abandoned quarry. At the front of the school close to the street is a bank of light gray volcanic rock, dacite, the same kind of rock involved in the eruption of Mount Saint Helens. The rock is fine-grained, with small crystals, which indicates that it cooled quickly at, or close to, the surface. Even more revealing, the mass of rock shows flow lines, indicating that while still molten at the surface, the syruplike mass spilled out over other portions of the quickly cooling rock, resulting in a failure to mix completely, something like the mixed doughs of a marble cake.

Incidentally, this rock mass also shows that the glaciers that much later slid south over New England passed over here. Sand in the ice gave the rock a polished surface. Near the top of the massive rock is a glacial groove, deeply gouged out by large rocks in the ice that moved across it. Glacial polishing, striations, and grooves are quite common on rock surfaces in New England. The fine parallel lines on the surface show the direction in which the great glacier was moving.

South of Boston at Atlantic Hill there is evidence of a volcano that erupted there long ago. Atlantic Hill is on the south side of a bay containing a number of islands. (These islands are glacial drumlins, hills of loose stones, sand and clay, carried south and overridden by glaciers.) A popular beach there, Nantasket Beach, is made of sand built up by waves during storms and serves to connect several of the glacial hills within the bay to the mainland at Atlantic Hill. On the south side of the low hill is a mass of hard black lava, composed of broken fragments of a lava flow, overrun and fused together by a fresh surge of lava. Such situations are common in lava flows in which the surface cools and hardens, then is fractured and engulfed by the continuing flow of molten rock.

East of Atlantic Hill, just offshore is a cluster of tiny islands consisting of hard, black rock, which apparently is all that remains of the once-active volcano, the source of the lava flow. At the foot of Atlantic Hill on the south side is a small ravine, a depression forming a straight line pointing toward the black rocks of the former volcano. The ravine is an eroded fault line, where the bedrock was broken by the mountain-building pressures that uplifted the mountains and lowered the Boston Basin. The east end of that fault-line depression is now inundated, forming Straights Pond.

At the fault, the south side was lifted while the north side was depressed to form the Boston Basin. Granite can be found on the south side of the fault. Sediments have filled the lower side so that it is now about as high as the other side. The uplifted granite still forms low hills on the southern side of Straights Pond.

Another kind of rock can be found near the shore where Nantasket Beach ends at Atlantic Hill. The rock is very fine-grained, almost glasslike, indicating that it cooled quickly at the surface, apparently a lava flow from the nearby volcano.

Farther from the shore at the northwest corner of Atlantic Hill there is a limited amount of still another kind of volcanic rock. It looks much like a dark, weathered sandstone but actually is volcanic ash packed and hardened into a compact mass somewhat reddish in color. The presence of volcanic ash indicates there was a violent explosion with great volumes of ash blown aloft, although only a small amount remains. The fine-grained felsitic rock close to shore is rock that resists internal pressures and can result eventually in a violent eruption. On the other hand, the lava by Atlantic Hill is the kind that flows freely; so it seems that like Mount Saint Helens and other volcanoes of the Cascades, this was a composite volcano and not always violent in its eruptions. The fault line of Straights Pond indicates that eruptions occurred along the fault, as eruptions often do.

How Erosion Has Shaped the Appalachians

The Appalachians have gone through profound changes. Over a vast expanse of time, the lofty mountains were worn down to a flat surface. Eventually that flat surface was uplifted to its present height; then further erosion again cut into the flat surface. Softer, less resistant rocks from the base of the once-lofty mountains were cut down to still lower levels, forming the rugged landscape we see today.

Just north of the Massachusetts border in southwestern New Hampshire is Mount Monadnock, not a very imposing mountain yet highly significant. It is representative of all the Appalachians as we see them today. From the road, looking out across the mountains, the skyline is uniformly flat, except for Monadnock, which stands above the common level. Quite

Outline of Rock Structure in the Appalachians of New England from Boston to Albany

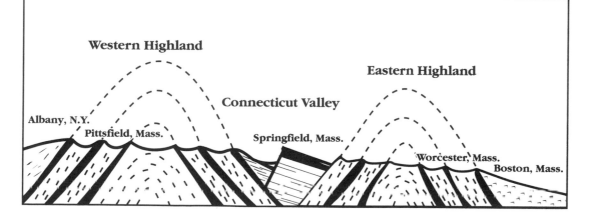

Western Highland

Eastern Highland

Connecticut Valley

Albany, N.Y.

Pittsfield, Mass.

Springfield, Mass.

Worcester, Mass.

Boston, Mass.

Mount Monadnock in New Hampshire is in a sense representative of all the Appalachian Mountains. The Appalachians have been worn down to a uniform height, except for Monadnock and others like it.

some time ago, geologists determined that the reason for the uniformity of the skyline in the Appalachians was prolonged erosion, which reduced the original mountains to an almost flat surface. Monadnock, although badly worn, was not completely flattened. Since the knowledge that the Appalachians were shaped by erosion was first deduced in relation to Monadnock, all prominences throughout the Appalachians, even the world, that stand above the common level of worn-down mountains are now termed *monadnocks,* the mountain in New Hampshire being the prototype of all such erosional remnants.

In the Appalachians many such monadnocks are known. The White Mountains of New Hampshire are obvious examples, including Mount Washington, the tallest mountain in New England. The White Mountains have resisted erosion because of their hard rock, granite. Other noteworthy monadnocks include Mount Katahdin in Maine, the Blue Hill south of Boston, and Stone Mountain near Atlanta, Georgia. Interestingly, Mount Monadnock itself has survived intense erosion, not because of especially hard rock formations, but apparently because of drainage patterns. It seems that water flowing away from that location cut down the surrounding areas, leaving Monadnock standing.

From the White Mountains of New Hampshire, U.S. Highway 2 follows the Androscoggin River eastward into the lowland areas of Maine, through extensive forests of spruce and fir, across numerous low ridges of hard rock. Those metamorphic rocks, altered and hardened by the forces that

Mount Katahdin in Maine, a monadnock, or erosional remnant. The term monadnock indicates it was formed as the surrounding mountains were worn away.

built the Appalachians, began deep within the mountains where heat and pressure were intense. With erosion they are now exposed at the surface. Some of the rocks are granite or similar types forced up from below as the mountains were uplifted. Gradually over a vast expanse of time the mountains were eroded, worn away. Mount Katahdin, a great mass of granite located in Baxter State Park north of Bangor, survives as a portion of the former mountain range that was not completely worn away, standing above the worn surface as a monadnock. Near Eastport and the adjoining province of Canada there are great masses of lava and volcanic ash, evidence of great, violent eruptions many millions of years before the last Ice Age.

Stone Mountain near Atlanta, Georgia, is a mass of granite that rose as the Appalachians were elevated. Hard, with a smooth surface, it has survived as other rocks about it have eroded.

Further evidence of Appalachian mountain building can even be found in suburban Boston on Beacon Street just beyond Boston College, where an inconspicuous bank of rock reveals folds and thrust faults. Here conglomerate rock sits above shale, though ordinarily the conglomerate at Boston is beneath the shale, wherever the two are found together. Conglomerate is made of gravel and looks much like concrete. Shale is a softer rock with fine, horizontal lines. On Beacon Street the rocks were folded as the mountains were built, and pressures were so intense that the rocks were actually overturned, leaving the conglomerate on top. Between the two kinds of rock is a line, a worn surface, actually a small thrust fault along which the harder conglomerate was shoved out over the

A thrust fault in Kentucky. Pressure from the east has shoved a mass of hard sandstone out over the less coherent rocks below. Such thrust faults are common throughout the Appalachians.

weaker shale. In the process of folding, the conglomerate was shoved upward to form the ridge that extends eastward along Beacon Street and Commonwealth Avenue to the edge of the Boston Basin.

The city of Boston is located on what was originally a peninsula; Washington Street extends down the middle of the peninsula. The stump of an old volcano was once found near Washington Street at the intersection with Grove Street. Buildings and paved streets now obscure the rocks, but evidence of volcanic activity can be seen in a quarry a few blocks south on Grove Street, where a dike of dark basalt indicates where molten rock once rose to the surface.

Beside Route 5 in central Massachusetts, north of Holyoke, are large dinosaur tracks on the east side of the highway. The Connecticut River is just beyond the dinosaur tracks, with Mount Tom Reservation on the west side of the highway. Mount Tom is at the southern end, the tallest portion of the Holyoke Range, a ridge of black rock, hardened upturned lava. Beyond Mount Tom are several deep notches in the otherwise uniform ridge of rock. At the level of each notch, rivers once flowed along the valley and gradually wore openings where their channels crossed the ridge. At that time the sandstone and shale of the lowland were as high as the ridge of rock, forming one continuous, flat surface across the valley. But the softer, less resistant sandstone and shale have been washed away, and the hard rock of the Holyoke Range now stands alone. Today no stream can flow across the ridge, except where the Connecticut River has been able to cut a notch as deep as the valley floor on each side. The gaps in the ridge show where streams once flowed and indicate how the valley has been deepened as the softer rocks have been worn away.

On the west side of Mount Tom is a ravine parallel to the range, visible from the road that skirts the western side of the Mount Tom Reservation. The ravine marks a fault line, along which sheets of lava that once covered the valley floor were broken and tilted upward to form the Holyoke Range. The hard, black volcanic rock now stands high above the ravine and slopes gradually away like the roof of a shed. The rock along the upturned steep edge has weathered, so that the bluff is no longer in the original

Dinosaur tracks on the left beside the Connecticut River, across the highway from Mount Tom, the highest peak of the Holyoke Range. Dinosaurs roamed here in the days when the mountains were being uplifted.

Dinosaur tracks formed in fine sand and mud from high mountains on each side of the valley. The ripple marks indicate the sediments sat in shallow water. The sand and mud have hardened to preserve the footprints in sandstone and shale.

position directly above the fault line. The broken rocks and soil along the fault have been washed away, leaving a ravine where the fault occurred.

A bit farther north, at South Deerfield, are the Sugarloaf Mountains—actually hills about 500 feet above the level of the valley. There are two hills composed of sandstone and conglomerate, rocks formed out of sand and gravel, respectively. The coarse rocks that have resisted erosion remain as hills after the weaker sandstone and shale of the surrounding valley have been washed away. The rocks of the Sugarloaf Mountains stand as remnants of a broad delta that once extended far out across the Connecticut Valley, formed by a stream off the adjoining highland. Mount Toby is another such mass of boulders and gravel now cemented together as solid rock. Toby is at the eastern edge of the Connecticut Valley where

The New River follows a meandering course across West Virginia. The meanders were established on the flat surface of the worn-down Appalachians and became entrenched as the land was uplifted. The skyline reveals the older, flat surface.

during the Triassic Period a swift stream carried gravel and boulders off the steep mountainside into the valley. In those days dinosaurs roamed across the lowland. The boulders were dumped at the foot of the mountains. But the tall mountains of the eastern highland are gone now, and the boulders of the stream bed stand alone—higher than what remains of the eastern highland. Erosion has gradually removed the highland and much of the valley surface. A modern stream, Roaring Brook, has cut into the base of Mount Toby and exposed the boulders there.

The New River now rises in North Carolina, but long ago it began farther east, no doubt somewhere in the mountains of Africa, before there was an Atlantic Ocean between the two continents. That old river developed a meandering course out across what was then a broad lowland, the quite flat, worn-down surface of the Appalachians. Such meanders are typical of lowland streams, for the current is not swift enough to cut a deep channel. Instead, bends develop as the current swings from one side to the other, developing a winding course across the flat lowland. The New River has maintained the lowland, meandering course despite the lowland being elevated, cutting down as fast as the lowland was being uplifted, thus forming what geologists call an *entrenched meander.* In spite of the name, the New River is not new. In fact it is older than the hills—older than the Appalachians! The New River had established its course across the flat surface of the worn-down mountains before these mountains were uplifted.

Upended strata of sedimentary rocks, originally horizontal. With the pressures of mountain building, a broad fold was arched upward; the top of the fold was then removed by erosion.

The Appalachians are most obviously folded at their midpoint, specifically in Pennsylvania and Virginia. Today in eastern Pennsylvania a series of parallel ridges with valleys in between indicate where sediment washed off the original lofty mountains into the Appalachian depression, forming layers of sand and clay in the lowland. Renewed pressure from the east caused the layers of sediment to fold as they were uplifted and shoved inland. Eventually, erosion of the uplifted surface cut away the tops of the larger folds, leaving only the almost vertical sides of the folded sediment. Then further erosion of the upended strata cut into the less resistant portion thus exposed. The sandstone had become quite hard, well cemented, resistant; consequently the upended strata of sandstone were left as ridges after the strata of shale had been eroded to form valleys. Some of the upended layers of rock were limestone, which is especially suseptible to erosion, for it readily dissolves in acid. Acidic water is common, inasmuch as decayed leaves and other vegetation form acid in water. So wherever a stratum of limestone was upended and exposed, a limestone valley was eventually formed. The most extensive example is the Great Valley, which stretches from Georgia northward through Pennsylvania. Some portions of the broad valley were formed from the erosion of shale, but the greater portion developed where limestone was dissolved and washed away.

When vegetation decays, carbon dioxide is formed. In the moist decaying leaves of a deciduous forest, the carbon dioxide combines with water to form carbonic acid. Although that acid is weak, there is an abundance of it from the decaying vegetation. The acidic water gradually dissoves limestone wherever it is exposed. In the Appalachian depression before the mountains were uplifted, much lime was deposited in the water. That lime became limestone, upended by the folding of the Appalachians, then eroded to form valleys.

Sandstone can be a very hard rock if the cementing material from the water is strong, but weak if the cement that holds the grains of sand together is weak. In some very hard, resistant sandstone the cement is silica, the same mineral as that of the sand itself. In other cases the cement may be iron oxide (rust), and the sandstone will crumble the way rust crumbles. Shale also varies in its resistance to weathering. Some shale is little more than dry clay from which it came, but in the heat and pressure of mountain building, chemical action may harden the shale, even converting it to slate. In general, though, sandstone is likely to be more resistant than shale. So where the upended rocks are exposed to erosion in Pennsylvania, the hard sandstone stands as ridges after the shale and limestone have crumbled and have been washed away. The sandstone ridges are likely to be quite uniform in height, matching the even surface level of the worn-down mountains, which we now see as the uniform skyline of eastern Pennsylvania. The Pennsylvania Turnpike was tunneled through a series of these ridges west of Harrisburg. The Tuscarora Mountains are one such ridge, Blue Mountain another. Altogether this series of massive ridges is known as the Allegheny Mountains. The Allegheny Plateau farther west also was uplifted, but not so severely folded and eroded.

Pinnacle Rocks State Park features this ridge of sandstone upended in the folding of the Appalachians of West Virginia. The remainder of a former arch has been lost to erosion, as have less resistant sedimentary rocks on each side.

Some smaller folds of stratified rock are still plainly visible in the western portion of Virginia. Also visible are upended strata, originally portions of larger folds, whose tops have been removed by erosion. In New England and eastern Canada the folding is not as evident. The massive igneous rocks there have been more resistant, yielding to thrust faulting with only minor folding. The Connecticut Valley was depressed by great faults along the highlands on each side. Boston Basin is another such depression, and farther north so is the lowland between New Brunswick and Nova Scotia.

When the original mountains were worn almost flat, the western side of New England was subsequently arched higher than the eastern, forming a slope toward the east. Therefore streams flowed eastward, cutting into the uniform surface, making stream valleys. The streams are gone now, but we can still see portions of their valleys. Eventually, tributary streams developed more or less at right angles to the eastward-flowing streams. Those tributaries flowed along the strata of upturned limestone and shale, hence cut down faster than the main stream flowing across more resistant rock. After a time, in what geologists call *stream piracy,* water flowing down the eastward slope was diverted into those branches. So although most of the original streams are gone, we still can see "notches" or "gaps" where the original streams flowed toward the east throughout the Appalachians.

In New England those remnants of former stream beds are called "notches." In the middle and southern Appalachians they are called "gaps"—wind gaps if that is all that flows through them now, or water gaps if a stream still flows through the opening in a ridge. Such gaps were used by explorers and pioneers when crossing the mountains to the West. Even today highways pass through the gaps, with travelers seldom realizing the source of each passageway. Wind gaps are more common, but some water gaps have survived. The Potomac and Shenandoah Rivers still merge to continue flowing across the Blue Ridge at a water gap in Virginia. The Delaware Water Gap is another prominent example.

In central Connecticut at New Britain there is an interesting example of a notch where a good-sized stream once flowed eastward down off the western slope, developing a channel along which Bristol and New Britain now are located. Just west of New Britain is a trap (basalt) ridge through which the swift river cut a channel. A wide road passes through there now. Unfortunately, a rock quarry has been cut into the ridge on one side of the road, obscuring the dimensions of the notch. From Bristol to the Connecticut Valley, the empty stream valley is quite large, though beyond New Britain in the Connecticut Valley there is no certain evidence to reveal what the course of the river may have been. One opinion holds that it continued across what is now the Connecticut Valley to the eastern highland at a point between Portland and Middletown, where the modern Connecticut River leaves the valley and follows a course toward the east in a channel cut deeply into hard rock. Why the modern river bends there instead of continuing directly south through the soft sediments of the valley has raised many questions. Inasmuch as the modern river diverges into the eastern highland where it is only 20 feet above sea level, the current would not have been swift enough to cut its deep channel. It seems plausible that the ancient stream that cut a channel into the western highland and the trap ridge at New Britain continued across the valley in an almost straight line to cut the channel in the eastern highland, a course that the modern river now follows.

The Blue Ridge and Piedmont Rocks of the Appalachians

Located in the middle section of the Appalachian Range today, the Piedmont consists of igneous and metamorphic rocks remaining from the base of the older Appalachians, much of which has drifted away with the continent of Africa. Beneath the sands of the adjoining coastal plain are more of these harder rocks at a lower level, worn down but not uplifted. Still more such rocks of the continental shelf are now covered by water offshore. Apparently these coastal rocks are what remains from the broad base of the older mountain range, much of which is now the Atlas Mountains of Africa. With the deep-seated pressures that built the mountains altered, causing the two continents to drift apart, the old rocks of the coastal region have remained at their lower levels. The cause of continental drift and mountain-building pressures is thought to be a ponderous circulation of rock under intense pressure at great depth. As time passes, convectional patterns can and seemingly do change. So instead of the two continents pressing together, they are drifting apart, going in opposite directions, Africa moving eastward and North America drifting toward the west, causing mountain building now on that coast.

The Blue Ridge is made of hard rocks similar to those of the adjoining Piedmont, Coastal Plain, and continental shelf. Evidently, as the two continents began to separate, waves on the intervening ocean tended to

Here, Piedmont rocks have been exposed. Piedmont is derived from the French for "foot of the mountain." The mountain is gone now, but the Blue Ridge stands above the Piedmont.

erode the rock surface remaining from the base of the old mountains. At that time it seems the Blue Ridge may have been the coastline, with the Piedmont and coastal rocks reduced by the waves to lower levels.

Today inland beyond the Blue Ridge are the Folded Appalachians, consisting of sediments in folded strata. On the Blue Ridge an elevated highway, Skyline Drive, follows the ridge, providing scenic views of the Piedmont and Coastal Plain on one side and the Folded Appalachians on the other. It is interesting that occasionally as motorists proceed smoothly along the crest of the ridge, they come to a dip in the highway and then out onto the level again. As elsewhere throughout the Appalachians, when the mountains were worn down to a common level, then elevated again, higher in the west, streams flowed off the slope toward the east. Those streams cut into the land, making valleylike depressions along their courses. Eventually tributary streams from each side developed deeper channels in softer strata so that the eastward-flowing streams were diverted into the lower channels. All that remained of the initial eastward course were gaps where the stream had cut channels, now abandoned. From the Blue Ridge such gaps in former eastward-flowing streams are readily evident. A series of gaps in harder strata often lead toward a dip in Skyline Drive, indicating that it too was made by a stream flowing down the eastward slope across the Blue Ridge.

Close to the Blue Ridge, on the western side, is the Shenandoah Valley. What is now the valley was formerly an upturned stratum of limestone with those eastward-flowing streams crossing it. Now, with the limestone eroded and gone, the Shenandoah River has been diverted to flow beside the ridge northward, where it merges with the Potomac and flows through a gap deep enough to maintain the eastward course. The empty dips in

A short way from Washington, D.C., the Potomac River flows off Piedmont rocks onto the sediments of the coastal plain, forming rapids known as the Great Falls of the Potomac.

Skyline Drive are now wind gaps, and the river flows eastward through a water gap.

Another interesting site in the Blue Ridge region, northeast of the Great Smoky Mountains and not far north of Asheville in North Carolina, is Mount Mitchell, the highest mountain peak in the East. It is a monadnock, highly resistant to erosion and made of quartzite, which originally was sand washed off the old Appalachians into an inner lowland. With further uplift of the Appalachians, the pressure partially melted grains of sand and fused them together, forming quartzite. The extremely hard quartzite has remained after all the less resistant rocks about it have eroded. Remarkably, what was once loose sand washed into the lowland has become the highest mountain in the East.

Until about the 1950s, geologists assumed there was a mountain range along what is now our east coast, just east of the Appalachians. As evidence, they cited signs of vast amounts of sediment washed off these mountains and deposited in what are now the eastern and midwestern states. That apparent mountain range was spoken of as "Old Appalachia." With so much sediment removed, it seemed that Old Appalachia finally was worn flat. Further evidence of the older mountain range was said to be the presence of granite and other such rocks, the base of the old mountains now gone. Although it is true that such rocks do exist in the Piedmont, beneath the sands of the coastal plain and underwater along the continental shelf, geologists have modified their interpretations. Such mountains did exist, but they have drifted gradually eastward with the continent of Africa.

Some of the mountains that provided the sediments have not departed with Africa. The Taconic Mountains of western Massachusetts provided much sediment now spread across the state of New York. Early in the Paleozoic Era, mountains were uplifted along a great fault line extending across what is now Pennsylvania northward along the depression of the Saint Lawrence River and beyond to the Gaspé Peninsula. Thrust faults and folded-rock formations remain as evidence of the tectonic activity bordering the south side of the Saint Lawrence Valley and the borders of New England. Beds of compacted ash throughout the East provide evidence of severe volcanic eruptions at the time.

Further disturbances in about the same region occurred later, near the middle of the Paleozoic Era. The revived activity was recognized first in eastern Canada, in Acadia; hence this interval of mountain building has become known as the Acadian Disturbance. The granite of the White Mountains rose at this time, as did that of Mount Katahdin in Maine. Similar granitic masses, batholiths, were formed in New Brunswick and Nova Scotia.

During these periods of mountain building, the Appalachian trough was further depressed as sediment washed into it from the adjoining mountains. The interior of the continent, farther inland, was very low during these times. Likewise, much of the East was under the water of a shallow inland sea. Sediments washed off the eastern mountains formed a broad delta, extending from Canada southward into Georgia. The Taconic Mountains of western New England provided much of the sediment, with more coming from streams off Old Appalachia, now the Atlas Mountains of Northwest Africa.

With the interior lands under water, much limestone, originally deposited as lime from the quiet waters, formed, later to be converted into marble by the pressures of mountain building, as in Vermont. Likewise, the mud washed into the lowlands hardened as shale, with some of it further converted to slate, while sand from the mountains became cemented as sandstone.

The Ouachita Mountains and Ozark Plateau

The Ouachita Mountains today extend from the Mississippi lowland through Arkansas into Oklahoma. In age and structure these mountains are much like the Folded Appalachians. During the early Paleozoic Era, while the Appalachian region was a lowland from the Gulf of Mexico northward through Canada into the North Sea, an extension of the depression reached westward into what is now Arkansas, Oklahoma, and Texas. Over a vast period of time, great depths of sediment washed into the southwestern depression. Study of these sediments reveals that they came from mountains that stood farther south, where the Gulf of Mexico sits today. In plate tectonics it is postulated that at one time in the distant past all the continents were joined as an immense landmass, termed Pangaea. Africa was contiguous with both North and South America, and Eurasia was in contact with Canada. There is much evidence to support this concept, in that geological formations of formerly adjoining continents are closely related, those of one appearing to be a continuation of the structures in another.

Here in Arkansas the Oachita Mountains have been folded upward by pressures from the south. This roadside view shows stratified rocks that have been tipped up on one side of a fold.

The Appalachians apparently end upon reaching the gulf states of the South. However, deep wells drilled through the sediments of the Gulf Coastal Plain find hard crystalline rocks from the roots of former mountains, indicating the original mountain range did not end in Alabama. Farther north, after the Appalachians were worn flat, further pressures elevated the worn surface of the mountain range to its present height, which is the height of the uniform skyline. In the South, however, instead of being uplifted, the worn surface sank to a lower level and was covered by the sediments of the Gulf Coastal Plain.

In Oklahoma the Ouachita Mountains overlie the older Arbuckle Mountains. Along the Texas border with Oklahoma are a series of these much older mountains: The Arbuckle, Wichita, and Amarillo Mountains form a line from southern Oklahoma into northwest Texas. These older mountains suggest that crustal disturbances in the region have a long history, an implication quite consistent with the concept of Pangaea and the plate tectonics theory. The remains of the Amarillo Mountains in the northwest end where they are scarcely visible. Close to the more recent Rocky Mountains, they now are covered by sediments of the Great Plains derived from the newer mountains.

In North America there are mountains in all stages of creation from initial growth to extinction. The Rocky Mountains were uplifted long ago, but the Appalachians and the Ouachita Mountains are even older and have gone through many changes. Still older are the former mountains of Oklahoma and northwest Texas, of which few now remain. The oldest of all, readily visible, are what remain from the stumps of former mountains in central Canada, the Canadian Shield.

In the East, the pressures of the African continent impinging on the coast compressed the previously submerged area. Folding and thrust faulting converted the lowland sediments into the Appalachian Mountains. In a similar way, the sediments of the southwestern depression were compressed and uplifted to form the Ouachita Mountains. It seems that the mountainous land mass that yielded sediments to the southwestern depression was also the source of pressures that elevated the depressed area later to become the Ouachita Mountains of Arkansas and Oklahoma. Significantly, the Ouachita Mountains were uplifted at about the same time the Appalachians were built, near the end of the Paleozoic Era, which is also the time the extensive land mass, Pangaea, is believed to have broken apart into separate continents. Apparently, deep-seated convection currents that dragged the continents together shifted, as convection patterns do. Instead of the continents being pressed together, they began drifting apart. After the future Africa detached from the present-day east coast, the Atlantic Ocean filled the void. Likewise, it seems that at about the same time a land mass on the southern border of North America began drifting away. As the southern land mass withdrew, another opening was formed, and what would become the Gulf of Mexico filled with water. Though the evidence is not conclusive, it could well be that until Pangaea broke apart, South America was contiguous with North America, just as Africa was joined to America's east coast. In that case, the sediments of the Permian Basin of Texas must have come off the rugged mountains of Colombia and Venezuela, now situated beyond the Gulf of Mexico. Or perhaps the eroded materials came from mountains that are now a part of Central America. A large fault line exists just south of the Yucatan Peninsula and extends across the gulf south of Cuba. Movement along that fault could have displaced the mountains that produced the Permian sediments.

As the Gulf of Mexico filled with water, the adjoining Gulf Coastal Plain sank, forming a slope to the south and allowing sediments from the north to cover the slope. Like the gulf itself, the Mississippi lowland has been formed by subsidence, apparently a consequence of the removal of supporting pressure from the south. For a time the waters of the gulf spread far inland across what is now the Gulf Coastal Plain and even farther north along the Mississippi Valley where the subsidence was greatest. There is evidence that gulf waters once reached the foot of the Ouachita Mountains, and into what is now northern Alabama. The severe earthquakes that occurred in the Mississippi Valley almost 200 years ago, the New Madrid earthquakes, along with more recent tremors, indicate that the subsidence has not entirely ceased. Yet the gulf waters no longer cover the Southern Coastal Plain, which indicates that further subsidence in the gulf itself has drained the waters from the coastal plain.

Little Rock, Arkansas, is at the eastern end of the Ouachita Mountains where the Arkansas River emerges into the Mississippi lowland. From Little Rock (named for the site of a popular riverboat mooring) the Arkansas River crosses a broad lowland to merge with the mighty Missis-

Seashells in a bank in northern Alabama indicate the land was once low and the Gulf of Mexico extended farther north across the coastal plain to northern Alabama, where now there are hills.

Beach pebbles become worn and flattened as they are washed back and forth on sand. Stream pebbles are more rounded. The presence of beach pebbles in northern Alabama 200 miles from shore indicates the Gulf of Mexico once extended much farther to the north.

sippi. The lowland is a highly productive agricultural area. It seems probable that rocks of the Ouachita Mountains do not end at the edge of the valley but are depressed and covered by sediments of the Mississippi Delta, the floodplain of the river.

The hot springs at the resort city of that name, near Little Rock, indicates that the tectonic activity of the mountains has not entirely abated. Throughout the years, the Arkansas River has developed a course from the west across the mountains. The broad river valley is said to separate the folded mountains from the Ozark Plateau on the north side of the valley. Actually the Ozarks were uplifted at the same time by the same pressures that folded and uplifted the Ouachita Mountains, but being farther inland, the region was uplifted without serious folding. The elevation of the Ozarks is analogous to that of the Appalachian Plateaus. The rocks at the surface of the Ozarks are predominantly limestone, indicating a lowland origin. As in large areas of the Midwest, the lowland was under water and much lime settled out of the water, eventually becoming limestone. In the Ozarks, granite lies deep below the surface but is exposed at the northeastern edge of the plateau, forming the Saint Francois Mountains, which consist of weathered granite.

The Boston Mountains on the northern side of the Arkansas Valley form the southern edge of the Ozark Plateau. Before the valley developed, the Boston Mountains and the Ozark Plateau were a continuation of the Ouachita Mountains, a continuous uplift but with less folding. The Boston Mountains are the highest portion of the Ozark Plateau, with elevations gradually decreasing northward, farther inland, away from mountain-building pressures.

The Ozark Plateau is a domelike uplift extending 200 miles to the north, ending at the Missouri River. The plateau merges with the prairies of Kansas and Oklahoma on the west and is bordered by the Mississippi Valley on the east. In the southern, higher portions of the plateau, erosion has cut into the original flat surface, leaving it so rugged that the plateau often is referred to as the "Ozark Mountains." In addition to the abundant limestone, other lowland sedimentary rocks include some sandstone, shale, and flintlike chert. The quality of the soil, due largely to the rocky fragments of chert and the rough surface, has made the region inadequate for anything more than subsistence farming.

North of the rugged Boston Mountains, streams such as the White, King, and Osage Rivers have maintained their lowland, sinuous courses, cutting down the land as rapidly as the plateau about them was uplifted, thus becoming entrenched meanders while giving emphasis to the lowland origin of the Ozark Plateau.

The Ouachita Mountains south of the Arkansas Valley provide unmistakable evidence of mountain-building pressures from the south. The sediments out of which the mountains were built are coarser and thicker toward the south. The mountains consist of massive folded ridges, extending from west to east, indicating that the pressures that caused the folding came from the south. As the mountains were being elevated, upward folds (anticlines) became mountainous ridges. The downward folding in between (synclines) became valleys. Highways from north to south through the Ouachita Mountains go up and down, out of one valley climbing to the crest of the adjoining mountain, thence down into the next valley. Each elongated mountain is covered with a forest of pine trees. Those forested highlands are now part of the Ouachita National Forest. The valleys are mostly farmlands with small towns as community centers, such as Danville and Mt. Ida. Appropriately named is the settlement of Mountain Valley. Initially, streams like the Ouachita River followed the downfolds (synclines) between highlands on each side, widening and deepening the valley. No doubt the Arkansas River cut its wide valley in a similar way, separating the intensely folded mountains from the uplifted plateau. In terms of current plate tectonics it seems evident that the pressures that folded the mountains and uplifted the plateau came from a landmass located where the Gulf of Mexico is today.

5

MOUNTAINS AND GLACIERS

In northern states, snow is likely to be heavy each winter, especially in the mountains. Gradually that snow tends to become packed as hard as ice. In fact, the snow does become consolidated into ice, as anyone who has had to walk on slippery city sidewalks knows. Fortunately the warmer weather of spring melts the ice, but in the mountains where at high elevations the air remains cold and the snow deep, fields of ice remain from one winter to the next.

The Portage Glacier at the end of the Turnagain Inlet in Alaska. Snow on the mountain becomes packed and hardened as ice, which then slides down the mountain. A moraine of glacial rock has blocked the drainage, and meltwater has formed a lake.

Stones from the Nisqually Glacier on Mount Rainier occupy the glacial valley after the ice has melted back. With warmer weather, most glaciers melt faster than they advance.

When a great mass of ice accumulates on a steep mountainside, the ice begins to slide gradually down the slope, as a result of its own weight and gravity. Such a slowly moving mass of ice constitutes a mountain glacier. The tall volcanic peaks of the Cascades in the Pacific Northwest have numerous glaciers. The Nisqually Glacier on Mount Rainier is a good example. That glacier moves along a valley on the mountainside at about eight inches a day, gouging out the sides of the valley, making it wider, more rounded. Snow added to the head of the glacier serves to keep the glacier sliding down the valley. But as it moves down the mountainside, warmer air is encountered at lower elevations. Consequently the ice melts as rapidly as the glacier advances, so that the end of the ice tends to remain in the same place, the glacier seemingly motionless, even though the ice is still sliding forward.

MOUNTAINS AND GLACIERS

Owing to a warming trend in recent years, the Nisqually Glacier and others like it have been melting somewhat faster than the ice advances. As a result, the end of the ice is actually retreating, even though the ice inside the glacier continues to move forward. Although the Nisqually Glacier once extended down the mountainside close to the highway bridge, the end is now out of sight around a bend in the valley. The old highway bridge has been replaced by a new one, though the concrete footings on which the old bridge rested are still there to mark the spot. Standing on one of these and looking up the mountainside, one can no longer see the glacier, only the rounded valley where the ice used to be. The empty valley now is littered with boulders left behind by the melting ice.

Anyone who leaves the road and hikes up the gradual slope to the present end of the glacier will get a good view of the boulders and smaller stones, down to grains of sand. Many of these stones have become somewhat flattened and polished on one or more sides. Previously frozen in the ice, many of the stones were dragged along the bottom or sides of the valley, becoming worn as they also scraped away the sides of the valley. If they were jolted loose by an especially resistant bed of solid rock, then frozen in the ice again, more than one side became

A broad line of boulders in western Massachusetts, left behind by the glaciers that once covered New England. These stones were broken off bedrock farther north and left here when the ice melted.

flattened. The worn sides may even show striations, parallel scratches gouged into the surface of a stone and sometimes into the bedrock of the valley itself. Other stones deep within the mass of ice may have been unaffected. Some of those may have tumbled down onto the glacier and were carried along on the surface of the ice. Where the ice finally melted, the stones have remained, forming what is known as a *ground moraine,* stones of all sizes scattered along the otherwise empty valley. Such debris is termed *glacial till.* Where the end of the ice remained for a time at its farthest advance, glacial till accumulates to form a distinct ridge, a *terminal moraine.*

In California, east of San Francisco, the Yosemite Valley once was occupied by a glacier. There, a ridge of glacial till, a terminal moraine, formed a dam to block drainage from the valley. The water that backed up behind the dam became a lake, now gone. Sediment from the water gradually filled the glacial lake, forming the meadow that now occupies the flat valley floor. Glacial lakes and meadows are common wherever glacial deposits have blocked drainage.

In the days when a glacier occupied Yosemite, rocks in the ice scoured the sides of the valley, cutting them back to give the site a rounded, U-shaped contour typical of glaciated valleys. In cutting back the sides of

These boulders in eastern Massachusetts form a recessional moraine westward from Cape Ann, north of Boston. The trees have grown here since the ice melted away.

the main valley, the ends of several tributary valleys were removed, leaving what is called a *hanging valley*. Now the streams that flow in these valleys become waterfalls tumbling down into the steep-walled valley below. The spectacular Yosemite Falls tumbles down almost half a mile to the valley floor. Even the nearby Bridalveil Falls spills down about an eighth of a mile, creating a dense spray that suggested the falls' name. There is much to be seen at Yosemite National Park and other glaciated areas, including those of New England, New York, and such places as Glacier National Park in Montana.

New England Glacial Geology

From Portland, Maine, Highway 302 leads northwest from the rockbound Atlantic Coast into the White Mountains of New England. The highway crosses from Maine into New Hampshire and follows the Saco River into a rounded valley with rugged mountains on each side. The mountains are covered with dark green forests of spruce, fir, and hemlock, fringed with the lighter green of birch, maple, and oak—except where sheer cliffs of bare rock form the valley walls. In the middle of an early spring afternoon the gray rocks and green trees high on the mountains are bright with sunshine, while the depths of the valley are in shadows, the sun out of sight below the western wall. Here and there sheltered patches of snow remain on the ground as evidence of a long winter that recently has come to an end.

At Bemis Brook a side road leads off into the woods toward beautiful Arethusa Falls, where water plunges abruptly from the mountainside into the valley. In the distance at the head of the valley, Mount Washington can be seen standing above the adjoining peaks and ridges.

The big glacial valley forms a gentle curve leading north into the mountains. Beside the highway a mountain stream spills over glacial stones and then passes sedately through a quiet pool on its way to the Atlantic. Here Willey Brook empties into the river, and Willey Mountain forms the western edge of the valley. The tall mountain stands as a monument to the Willey family, lost in a rock slide off the steep mountainside.

The last few miles at the head of the valley are an abrupt climb into Crawford Notch. Gray rocks on each side form a slender corridor scarcely wide enough for the highway and the stream beside it. At the summit, the narrow gap opens abruptly into an irregular tableland surrounded by mountains. On the right is Saco Lake, and beyond it a fine view of the Presidential Range, the highest mountains of the northern Appalachians.

A cog railway, more than a century old, forms an almost straight line up the side of the tallest peak, Mount Washington. The mountain is 6,288 feet tall. At more than a mile high, the summit stands well above the timber line, forming a gray mass silhouetted against a background of bright blue sky and white clouds. At its base the mountain is surrounded by the green of the forest. While snow covers the land, the White Mountains are well named.

In New England the winters are long. But at least a million years ago the Earth became colder than it is today. Much of the snow that fell during the winter failed to melt during cool summers and so remained on the ground from one year to the next. Gradually the snow became a hard mass of ice that covered virtually all of what is now Canada and northern portions of the United States. Where the snowfall was heavy, great depths of ice accumulated. One such area was near Hudson Bay, where a tremendous mountain of ice developed. Because of its height, the great mass of ice began to spread outward like snow sliding off a roof. Slowly but with the force of a moving mountain, the ice spread outward in all directions, much of it southward across the Appalachians of New England and New York into parts of Pennsylvania and New Jersey. Ice covered North America as far south as the Ohio and Missouri Rivers. In the Far West, snow covered the mountains and ice extended into the valleys.

For a million years or so, extensive glaciers covered the North. At intervals the ice would melt away, but later it would spread out over the land again. Not only North America but northern Europe and Siberia were buried under mountains of ice. Even today Antarctica and most of Greenland are covered. Glaciers remain in the mountains of Alaska, western Canada, and the Pacific Northwest. The glaciers have disappeared from the Appalachians, yet abundant evidence remains.

The summit of Mount Washington can be reached by means of the cog railway from the west or by road up the eastern side. The top of the mountain is a somewhat rounded surface of hard rock littered with boulders. On the bleak, windswept surface, clumps of stunted plants struggle for a foothold among the rocks. Because of the elevation, the air is cold, the wind severe. Although granite is more common in the White Mountains, the solid rock at the top of Mount Washington is a fine-grained schist—a dark rock with small, flat crystals of mica that glisten in the light.

MOUNTAINS AND GLACIERS

Many of the boulders on the broad surface of the mountain have been worn and polished, flattened on the sides. Weathered stones are common in the fields of New England, as well as on the top of Mount Washington, evidence that massive glaciers once covered the land, even the highest mountains of the region. Rocks broken off farther north are left scattered everywhere when the ice finally melted. Farmers have cleared many of the stones from their fields and stacked them in rows to serve as stone fences. Larger boulders remain where the melting ice left them. Where a field is especially stony, it may be left as grass for cattle. Bushes and trees often grow up among the boulders, obscuring them from view. Such boulders, moved south by the ice, are called "erratics." The term *erratic* implies that the boulder is out of place, moved by the glacier.

Glacial boulders are common throughout New England. An especially well known erratic is Ship Rock in South Peabody, near Route 128 north of Boston. The curving sides of Ship Rock have been scoured and shaped by friction with the bedrock it was shoved over by the ice. The Bartlett Boulder, located in the woods south of Bartlett, New Hampshire, is another noted example. Deep grooves have been scoured into the sides of the huge boulder, for in its position under the ice it was shoved a long way over solid rock. The largest erratic in New England, the Madison

This is an especially large glacial erratic in the Cape Ann recessional moraine. Notice the broad groove worn into the top of the boulder before it was dislodged and shoved south by the glacier.

Here in suburban Boston a deep groove has been gouged in hard bedrock by stones imbedded in glacial ice moving over it.

Boulder, is in a New Hampshire forest southwest of Conway. The Madison Boulder is as large as a good-sized house: approximately 25 feet wide, 83 feet long, and 37 feet high. That massive granite erratic was broken from a ledge two miles farther north. It provides ample evidence of the force with which ice scoured the surface of New England.

Many of the glacial stones at the top of Mount Washington are either granite or gneiss, not at all like the solid rock of the mountain itself. But rock surfaces to match the boulders can be found somewhat farther north. The worn and polished boulders were broken off rock formations in the north and brought to the moutaintop by the glaciers moving across the land.

At several locations on Mount Washington the solid rock has been polished and scratched by the ice moving across the top of the mountain, forming striations. Ice itself is not hard enough to scratch the rocks, but glaciers generally contain much sand and gravel, which act as abrasives. Deep striations likewise can be seen on the rocks at the top of Mount Mansfield, the tallest peak in Vermont. Such lines on mountaintops show that the continental ice was moving from the northwest, the direction of the "scratches." For the great glaciers to have covered the mountaintops

Sand and rock in the ice polished the bedrock as the ice moved across it. Rocks in the ice also have scratched parallel lines, striations, all oriented in the direction the ice was moving.

of New England, the massive ice must have been both broad and more than a mile deep. With the center of the ice cap about 700 miles farther north, the mountain of ice must have been even greater in Canada, perhaps two miles high.

Now, on a clear day, the top of Mount Washington affords a fine view of the Appalachians. As one looks out across the rugged surface of New England, it is hard to imagine what the the land looked like when ice covered everything in sight. Had anybody been there to see it, the view would have been much the way Greenland appears today—ice as far as the eye can see, a flat surface sloping gradually to the south.

Until Louis Agassiz came to America from Switzerland in 1846, nobody in New England knew why there were so many stones in the fields there. The evidence of glaciation was everywhere, but kames and drumlins were just hills, even to the people who lived on them. As a native of Switzerland, Agassiz was familiar with moraines, glaciated stones, and the outwash from melting ice. As a naturalist at Harvard University he noticed what other people were likely to ignore as meaningless. Wherever solid rock was exposed at the surface, Agassiz could see that the rock had been polished by masses of glacial ice sliding over it. The parallel lines often found on the surface of bedrock were also recognizable to him as the grooves and striations worn by hard stones in the ice sliding across the surface, a familiar sight in the Alps. Those lines all pointed in a more or less northerly direction, revealing to him the direction from which the great ice sheets had moved. Agassiz was fascinated with the evidence of massive ice that had covered everything everywhere in New England, a glacier far more extensive than those of the alpine valleys with which he had been familiar.

The enthusiasm Agassiz engendered has continued to this day. Now we all can see the great boulders moved by the ice, the striations carved into solid rock, even on the tops of mountains. In Canada where great mountains of ice accumulated and slid south, the rocks from ancient mountains have been scoured, worn down, and exposed as a bare surface visible even from the Trans-Canada Highway.

The Terminal Moraine

The moving ice of the great glaciers scraped away soil, bushes, and stones, leaving behind a scratched and polished surface of bare rock. Huge boulders were torn from steep ledges. Weaker rock was crushed to form sand and clay. The ice that had been crystal clear gradually became dark with the clay and bits of rock it contained. To the Stone Age men hunting mammoths near its southern edge, the great mass of ice must have appeared as a dusky, drab mountain of frozen clay and stone with white snow on top.

For more than a million years the ponderous mass of the continental glaciers continued moving over the mountains into warmer lands farther south. The movement was slow but persistent, though the leading edge of the ice appeared not to move at all, for melting was as rapid as its forward movement. Like a conveyor belt in a factory, the glacier continued to slide forward, yet ended in the same place. Stones within the mass were dumped where the ice melted, forming a great, long heap of boulders, gravel, sand, and clay at the southern end. Today the ice is gone, but a ridge of boulder clay remains where the glacier ended. Such a ridge at the end of a glacier is called a *terminal moraine*.

The Long Island moraine, from Brooklyn to Montauk Point, is bordered on the south by a sand plain built by meltwater from the glaciers. Sand from the melting ice makes a broad beach that slopes from the ridge to the water's edge and beyond. About 20,000 years ago, the edge of the continental ice stood at the middle of Long Island. Heaps of rock were dumped where the ice melted. Meltwater carried away the finer particles of sand and clay, spreading them out beyond the end of the glacier. Those finer particles now form the broad surface of Hempstead Plain, an *outwash plain*.

When the melting ice retreated to what is now the northern shore of Long Island, and while the northern branch was being built, meltwater carried away sand and clay to form another outwash plain. The Brookhaven National Laboratory, a nuclear research center, is located on that flat surface of sand between the two branches of the terminal moraine.

The northern ridge of Long Island can be traced underwater from Orient Point to Cape Cod. From Buzzards Bay to Orleans on the cape the moraine is a massive ridge of glacial material deposited where the ice ended. The terminal moraine is bordered on the south by a sandy outwash plain sloping to the ocean shore. Highway 6 follows the ridge eastward and provides a good view of the cape. At the far end of Long Island, each ridge becomes a finger pointing toward the east. Looking at a map, we see that Block Island, Martha's Vineyard, and Nantucket are islands on a continuation of one ridge. The other branch of the terminal moraine points toward Fisher's Island and the Rhode Island shore. At Westerly, Rhode Island, many large boulders mark the terminus of the ice. Still farther east, the ridge becomes Cape Cod. The tremendous bulk of Long Island and Cape Cod provides impressive evidence of glaciation. The mountain of ice must have been truly massive to have built so great a moraine at its southern edge.

What is now Long Island Sound, between Long Island and southern New England, was formerly but a stream valley along which water flowed eastward to the ocean beyond. Long Island then was but a portion of the low coastal plain. The island today consists of whatever the ice scraped from the land farther north in New England. Located on the smooth surface of the outwash plain are the southern portions of Brooklyn, Kennedy Airport, and numerous towns, such as Hempstead. The smooth surface does not end at the water's edge. As anyone bathing at Coney Island or other Long Island beaches can testify, the gentle slope continues far out into the water, even though waves have built ridges of sand to modify the slope and form beaches, such as Long Beach and Jones Beach.

Inasmuch as the continental glaciers extend far to the west, the terminal moraine continues westward also, from Brooklyn across the southern edge of Staten Island, thence northwestward near Plainfield and Morristown, New Jersey, toward Stroudsburg, Pennsylvania. The moraine continues westward along an irregular course, the variations depending largely upon the roughness of the Appalachians.

The New Jersey city of Plainfield is appropriately named, as it is situated on a glacial outwash plain. Just to the north of the terminal moraine in that state, the great glacier scooped out rocks and soil to form depressions in some places and dumped the excavated material in other places, blocking the drainage. Consequently lakes formed in the depressions. Traveling through northern New Jersey, or simply looking at a map of the state, one can see that small ponds and larger lakes are abundant, whereas south of the glaciated area we find few such bodies of water. With the glacier blocking normal drainage, a great lake at one time covered much of the area. As happens with such lakes, sediment washing into the glacial lake settled to the bottom, making the water increasingly shallow. Now, some portions of the once-broad lake have become filled and are simply swamps. Others have filled completely, forming open fields, flat meadows covered with grass.

Leaving New York City by way of the Lincoln Tunnel, we soon come to a broad area of swamps and meadows in New Jersey, remnants of the former glacial lake. Another such area of ponds, swamps, and meadows is encountered by continuing in a northwesterly direction. Located west of Paterson, New Jersey, between Routes 23 and 80, the region is largely undeveloped, except where the meadows have become golf courses; the ponds are now city reservoirs, and the swamps are wildlife preserves.

Visitors to New York City can readily find evidence of the glacier that covered Manhattan. Large boulders left behind by the ice can be seen in Central Park and at the Zoological Park in the Bronx, which rests on solid rock polished by the glacier that passed over it. Parallel lines, striations, gouged into the exposed bedrock can be seen in Central Park and elsewhere in banks of rock, including the south side of Riverside Drive near 200th Street.

Evidence of Glaciation in New England

The great glacier moved farther south along the lowland that is now Narragansett Bay. Consequently the end moraine is farther south out of sight under the waters of Rhode Island Sound. Likewise, a lobe of ice moved south along the lowland that is now Buzzard's Bay so that the moraine there is also under water. The portion of Cape Cod that extends northward from Eastham to Pilgrim Heights was formed by outwash from the glacier into a void in the ice. If Cape Cod can be likened to an arm, with Chatham at the elbow, it is evident that the upper arm is built of outwash material in layers, rather than directly by the ice. At North Truro and Provincetown where the wrist bends toward the bay, the peninsula has been shaped more recently by ocean waves and so has the form of a sand spit. At South Wellfleet, Marconi erected his wireless station to signal across the Atlantic Ocean and thus demonstrate that wireless telegraphy, which preceded the development of radio, could broadcast signals across great distances. The broad area of sand in layers on which he had his station is no longer as broad as it was in 1902. The flat surface then extended about 160 feet farther east. Ocean waves have cut into the soft sand and have scattered it along the shore to form the curving sand spit on which Provincetown now is located. Those ocean waves that cut back the heights also built the broad beaches of the National Seashore and with help from the wind developed some conspicuous sand dunes. Farther south, a ridge of sand forms a barrier beach to enclose Pleasant Bay between East Orleans and East Harwich. The sand from the heights at South Wellfleet and from what was an eastward extension of the cape has been spread even farther south to build Monomy Island, now a national wildlife refuge.

Along the south shore of Cape Cod the outwash plain provides many sandy beaches. At Dennis Port, for example, the sand slopes gradually to the water. The gradual slope of the outwash plain continues far out under the water. At Woods Hole, waves have cut into the outwash plain to form an abrupt sea cliff that provides a good view of the innumerable layers of sand that elsewhere lie underfoot, out of sight. Similar views of what lies below the surface of the cape can be found in the east along the Atlantic shore from South Wellfleet to Chatham, where waves have cut into glacial deposits. A broad view of the cape can be obtained from a watchtower located on the moraine beside Highway 6: the broad and massive undulating ridge of the moraine itself, Cape Cod Bay in the north, the broad outwash plain to the south, and the waters of Nantucket Sound beyond.

Driving north from New York City to New England, we enter the Connecticut Valley. There at the edge of New Haven, Route 15 leads through a tunnel cut into West Rock, a kind of rock referred to locally as *trap*. The massive West Rock stands prominently above the valley floor. Originally it was molten rock forced up from below, which hardened before reaching the surface, but since then the surrounding shale and sandstone have been worn away, leaving the hard rock standing high above the valley floor.

A short way beyond West Rock, Route 10 leads north toward Mount Carmel. Not far beyond the town is the mountain itself, commonly known as "Sleeping Giant," because of its appearance. Mount Carmel is another mass of trap rock. The head of Sleeping Giant lies toward the west, close to Route 10. Here, a highway and a small stream, Mill River, pass through a narrow gap, cut before the Ice Age by a larger stream. That ancestral Farmington River flowed through the gap on its way to the valley that is now Long Island Sound. As the glacial period was coming to an end, a mass of ice, stones, and dirt blocked the narrow gap, serving as a dam at Mount Carmel. The waters of the stream backed up to form a lake north of the obstruction. The depth of the water in that lake is indicated by terraces on the surrounding hills.

Continuing northward on Route 10, along the pre-glacial river channel, we find evidence of other glacial dams at Cheshire, and near Southington.

Water in each case backed up behind the obstructions, forming lakes. At Cheshire the lake finally emptied to the east, cutting a new channel through a sandstone ridge at South Meriden, a channel that the Quinnipiac now follows. Terraces on the surrounding hills indicate that the lake here became quite deep before rising high enough to find an outlet and cut a new channel. The moraine at Southington once extended across the entire Connecticut Valley to New Britain and nearby Rocky Hill. Outwash from that moraine built a sand plain with finer clay beyond, as at Berlin, a town south of New Britain. (As with the glacial clay at other locations, the clay at Berlin has been used for making bricks.) North of the moraine the Connecticut River was impounded to form a large lake extending far to the north. The water level of the lake rose high enough to pour over the obstruction, developing a spillway in the lowland just east of New Britain. The lake has since emptied, but a small creek still flows through the spillway.

Plainville is a small town west of New Britain and north of the glacial obstruction, the moraine at Southington. There the Farmington River, flowing from the north, with its channel blocked at Southington, emptied great volumes of sand into a glacial lake, building the flat surface that gives Plainville its name. Still farther north the flat, level surface continues through the town of Farmington and far to the north. That flat surface, a result of the sediment that gave the lake a smooth bottom, now reveals the extent of the glacial lake. Eventually the water in that lake rose high enough to find an outlet to the east through the trap ridge that had been confining it. The ridge apparently had been broken along a fault line, and the rushing water gradually cut a gorge to completely empty the glacial lake. The Farmington River, once impounded at the glacial lake, today flows south to Farmington and then bends and flows northward to the gorge and the Connecticut River beyond. The former channel of the Farmington River, running past Sleeping Giant south to Long Island Sound at New Haven, remains obstructed. South of the obstruction at Cheshire, the small Mill River now follows the old channel; the middle portion of the former channel is now drained by the Quinnipiac flowing south to Long Island Sound and by the Pequabuck flowing eastward and then northward, emptying into the Farmington.

An even more spectacular glacial diversion affected the Merrimac River in Massachusetts. The Merrimac still flows south through Nashua, New Hampshire, to Lowell, Massachusetts; beyond there the channel was once obstructed by glacial deposits left by melting ice. With the old southward channel no longer open, the river was diverted to the northeast across several ridges of hard rock. Waterfalls developed at those ridges where the water tumbled over to lower levels. The early settlers soon harnessed the falling water to turn waterwheels as a source of power. Industries developed at each waterfall, and cities then grew up where the industries were, giving New England its start as an industrial region. Those cities, Lowell, Lawrence, and Haverhill, have long histories as manufacturing centers.

Although the Merrimac River has been diverted, the pre-glacial channel south to Boston remains plainly evident. A line of lakes and ponds now occupies the old river valley on the outskirts of Boston, notably Horn Pond, the elongated Mystic Lakes, Spy Pond, and Fresh Pond. The Mystic Lakes are drained by the Mystic River, which flows away from the old channel southeastward into Boston Harbor. These glacial lakes and the old Merrimac channel can be seen from Route 3, which runs north out of Boston, past Fresh Pond, then along the west side of the Mystic Lakes and north to Lowell and the Merrimac River. Route 2, bearing northwest from Boston, passes between Spy Pond, plainly visible on the right, and Little Pond close by on the left.

Immediately south of the ponds is the Charles River. The Charles, flowing northeast, abruptly bends to follow the old Merrimac channel southward a short distance to the Back Bay section of Boston. There the Charles turns away to the east-northeast into Boston Harbor. The pre-glacial Merrimac continued through the Back Bay of Boston and the lowland of South Boston into what is appropriately named the Old Harbor. The Back Bay is no longer a bay but has been filled as the city expanded. However, the former channel is still low land, except where glacial deposits formed an obstruction.

Route 128, a circumferential highway around metropolitan Boston, has become famous in some quarters because of the enterprising scientific research and development establishments now located along the route. The broad highway begins in the north at Gloucester, a small city on the coast famous as a fishing port. Rockport, a neighboring town, is equally famous, as an artist colony. Gloucester and Rockport are located on Cape Ann, a broad prominence extending out from the North Shore. A prominent recessional moraine can be readily traced from Cape Ann westward along Route 128 as far as Lexington. At Lexington, there are boulders of the moraine along the south side of Route 128, just north of the city on the outwash plain. That outwash is readily evident in the swampy lowlands at the southern edge of town.

Beyond Lexington the moraine continues in a southwesterly direction along the north side of Route 20 out of Boston. Here in Weston, Wayland, and Sudbury along the north side of Route 20 a good view of the moraine can be obtained by driving through this suburban area. Bordered by stone fences, the roads curve gently beneath overhanging trees that have grown up out of the boulder-strewn surface of the recessional moraine.

The retreating ice front must have stood for quite some time across Massachusetts, judging by the prominence of the moraine. Evidence of the Cape Ann Moraine can be found at irregular intervals along a curving line across the state, close to Routes 20 and 90. Portions of moraines with outwash plains can be found south and west of Worcester in lowlands bounded by Route 20 on the south and Route 2 in the north, where there is an abundance of rounded glacial hills, called drumlins. Drumlins are made entirely of glacial till: a mixture of stones in various sizes, from boulders to gravel, sand, and clay. The glacial till in a drumlin is the same unsorted mixture found in moraines, and the similarity is significant. End moraines are formed where the ice front remains more or less in a fixed position with movement within the ice carrying more and more stones, sand, and clay to be added to the accumulation where the ice finally melts. It seems that on some occasions a glacier would resume its advance, riding up over the moraine already deposited and creating the smooth outlines of a drumlin, somewhat like half an egg or an inverted spoon. In rising up over the morainal material, the ice would be jolted up over the obstacle, then slope more gradually down the leeward side. Drumlins are steep on the northern side, the direction from which the glacier was moving, but slope more gently toward the south. Perhaps the reason we find only scattered evidence of the recessional moraine west of Worcester is because the glacier built a series of moraines and then advanced over them, leaving drumlins instead.

It seems a similar sequence of events may have occurred in the Boston Basin, for drumlins are abundant there, too. Though all drumlins tend to be smooth, oval-shaped hills, longer in the direction the ice was moving, not all are exactly alike. A few are almost round, but most are at least twice as long as they are wide. Boston has a great number of hills, almost all drumlins. An appreciable share of them are islands in the harbor or along the shore. The absence of stratification lines indicates the drumlins were formed directly by the glacier, not by meltwater from the ice. Drumlins vary in size as well as in shape, and many are quite large. The highest in and around Boston, at 340 feet above sea level, is Lyman Hill in Brookline. Among the better known are Beacon Hill, Bunker Hill, and the nearby Breeds Hill, memorable as the scene of a Revolutionary War battle. Parker Hill is located close to Route 9, where that highway enters Boston from Brookline. This drumlin is conspicuous and convenient for inspection in that an excavation on the west side has exposed the till of which drumlins are made.

South and east of Boston, toward Nantasket Beach, drumlin islands sit in the harbor. Atlantic Hill at the southern end of Nantasket Beach is solid rock, but the beach extends north to a drumlin, Great Hill, revealing glacial till of all sizes from boulders to fine clay, with no lines of stratification. Many of the boulders from the drumlin ring the foot of the hill. Still others are on the north side at the appropriately named Stony Beach, moved there by the same waves that cut back the end of the drumlin. Those waves also moved the glacial material that now connects Great Hill with two other drumlins due west at the town of Hull. Some of the finer sand was carried still farther west, connecting two more drumlins to form a single island. The view from Great Hill reveals numerous other drumlins in the harbor. South of Great Hill, Nantasket Beach itself has connected a series of drumlins, and directly to the west is a peninsula with two. Enclosed by Nantasket Beach and its extension westward are the waters of Hingham Bay, where we find a few more drumlins.

Clearly, there is no shortage of drumlins in Boston and the adjoining bays. During the Ice Age when they were built, the present harbors were dry land, a coastal plain. That plain extended many miles to the east to include what is now the Georges Banks fishing grounds out beyond Boston Harbor. The fossil bones and teeth of Ice Age elephants, mastodons and mammoths, have been found there in recent years where those animals roamed during the glacial period. In those days the Boston Basin and harbor were simply an inner portion of the coastal plain.

In the Roxbury section of Boston, just south of Parker Hill is the aptly named Jamaica Plain. In the midst of the plain is a large pond, Jamaica Pond. Jamaica Plain is a glacial outwash plain, with some gravel, but mostly covered by sand and fine silt. The outwash apparently came from

A glacial kettle hole with a small kame in the background, formed after a block of ice was left by a retreating glacier. Sand filled in around the block of ice, and as it melted, a cavity was left in the glacial outwash. This kettle hole has filled with water.

a recessional moraine, but there is none in the immediate vicinity, which suggests that the ice front advanced over the morainal material previously deposited and converted it into the drumlins of the Boston Basin. Later the front retreated and stood north of the Boston Basin while building the conspicuous Cape Ann Moraine.

Farther south along the coast toward Cape Cod are the cranberry bogs of eastern Massachusetts. These bogs are round kettle holes that have become partially filled with damp, spongy soil ideal for growing cranberries.

Jamaica Pond, like the cranberry bogs, is a kettle hole. Kettle holes are common in glaciated areas, especially in glacial outwash plains, and are formed as a glacier retreats. With a glacier melting rapidly, a crevasse often develops, very likely the result of a ridge of hard rock straining the ice sheet, causing it to crack. Melting along the crack widens the crevasse.

A glacier in Alaska. Note the stream emerging from beneath the ice. Meltwater from the surface falls through a crevasse. Warm water opens up a cavern beneath the ice, and a stream there gradually builds up a stream bed of rounded gravel beneath the ice.

Ice at the surface of the glacier, exposed to the sun and warm air, melts and then flows south along the surface, plunging into the crevasse. This warm water further widens the crevasse. This process continues until the crevasse becomes a broad space separating the glacier from a block of ice isolated to the south. Meltwater continues to flow from the glacier, carrying with it much sand and other sediment until a sand plain, or outwash plain, builds around the island of ice. Whatever its original shape, the ice left behind tends to become rounded, due to the more rapid melting of any corners or jagged edges. By the time the ice island completely melts, the end of the retreating glacier has melted back so far that meltwater no longer carries sand far enough to fill the rounded hole where the block of ice had been, and a kettle hole is formed. Some kettle holes become filled with water, but with porous sand at the bottom; many others remain dry, as did one across a side street from Jamaica Pond.

Eskers

South of Jamaica Pond across Jamaica Plain is the Arnold Arboretum. There, inside the park, is a ridge of gravel on which trees now are growing, known as an esker. Eskers are the beds of streams that flowed in caverns beneath glacial ice. In mountain glaciers, meltwater from the surface of a glacier sometimes will flow into a crevasse or into a hole at the edge of the valley. The warm surface water may then open up a cavern at the base of the ice forming a stream that can flow beneath the glacier. That stream will deposit enough sand and gravel along the way to build a typical stream bed within the ice cavern. Eventually, when the ice is gone, the sand and gravel of the stream bed will remain. With the ice that confined it gone, the stream bed will stand above its surroundings as a winding ridge of gravel, something like an abandoned road bed. Eskers ordinarily are quite level on the surface but may wind from side to side.

Close to the esker in the arboretum are two well-rounded kames, also formed while ice still covered the land, also with the formation of a crevasse in a glacier. As meltwater from the surface carries sand into the

Meltwater from glacial ice has carried away sand and deposited it here in Maine. Such beds of stratified sand are known as *kames*. The sand was worn off bedrock by the glacier passing over it.

A glacial hill, or kame, in a Boston park, formed of sand washed from the ice into a rounded opening in the melting glacier. The trees grew here after the ice melted.

opening, the warm water widens it, causing it to become rounded where water pours into the opening. More and more sand is carried into the opening and takes the rounded shape of that opening. Eventually, after all the ice disappears, the rounded, cone-shaped mass of sand remains as a kame.

The shape of a kame is determined by the shape of the opening in the ice; hence not all kames are round. However, all kames do tend to be stratified, or in layers, as are all sediments deposited out of water. The presence of stratification and the fact that the mound is composed of virtually nothing but sand and some stream-rounded gravel will indicate that a hill is a kame. If the current was swift, a kame may have some strata of gravel, but sand is more common. (In contrast, a drumlin consists of a mixture of glacial till with rarely any lines of stratification.)

Another obvious esker can be found at Edmunds Park in Newton. The end of this esker has been cut back to obtain gravel and reveals the rounded pebbles of the former stream bed. This esker extends southwestward to merge with an outwash plain in Newton. There the stream emerged from a cavern beneath the ice to spread sand over a broad surface.

Farther north in Maine, eskers are many miles long. They also are broad and high, indicative of large streams beneath the great glacier. Many of the eskers in Maine are so massive that they have been used as the foundations on which to build roads.

In Connecticut, Job's Pond in a sand plain east of Portland is perhaps the most noted kettle hole in the area. Other such kettle holes nearby were formed as described, with sand filling in around blocks of melting ice, but many are dry, well-rounded depressions rather than ponds. Kames can be seen in an area northwest of Lamentation Mountain, a prominence northeast of Meriden, but there are many others throughout New England. As the great mass of ice melted back along the edges of the Connecticut Valley, meltwater washed into the open space between the remaining ice and the sides of the valley. Those stratified deposits along the valley walls remain as kame terraces. Such kame terraces can be examined wherever the stratified sand is exposed. From above, the terrace appears somewhat flat, like an outwash plain, perhaps pitted with dry kettle holes. But at lower levels the kame terrace can be easily distinguished from the valley wall of solid rock.

Glaciation in the State of New York

Evidence of glaciation is readily apparent throughout New York State. South of Utica on Route 8 are some conspicuous kames where openings in the ice have been filled by meltwater carrying sediment. Some of the kames have been cut open for the sand and gravel they contain. The gravel in some of these kames indicates that water issued from glacial caverns with sufficient velocity to move some good-sized stones.

In the Adirondacks as in the Connecticut Valley, kame terraces along the valley walls are common. Meltwater has deposited sand in the spaces where glaciers melted back from the sides of valleys. Dwindling valley glaciers were common in the Adirondacks as warmer weather brought the Ice Age to an end.

Well-formed drumlins are also plentiful in northern New York, east of Rochester, between Route 90 and Lake Ontario. There the the great glacier apparently advanced over previously deposited morainal material to form drumlins out of the overridden till. Somewhat farther south, lobes of ice advanced along a number of river valleys where water had flowed north until obstructed by the ice. The moving ice scoured out those valleys, leaving them round and deep. Those glaciated valleys later filled with water and became the Finger Lakes. While scouring out the river valleys, the ice accumulated a mass of glacial stones, sand, and clay, forming the Valley Head Moraines where the ice finally melted. Although the streams had previously flowed northward, they no longer could, for their lower valleys had been filled with till, in bulldozer fashion, by the advancing glacier. With the moraine blocking drainage to the south, a newer drainage pattern for the lakes was developed in a devious course eastward to Syracuse, then northward to Lake Ontario at Oswego.

South of the Valley Head Moraines and eastward to the Catskills the region now drains into the Susquehanna River. Today in the upper reaches of this river and its tributaries, the valley floors contain large amounts of glacial outwash, forming what geologists call *valley trains*. Sediments from the glacier filled the valley floors, making a flat surface, which was then cut into by more recent stream action. Remnants of what had filled the valley now remain as terraces along the sides of the valleys. Ideal examples can also be seen from the Alaskan Railroad between Anchorage and Mount McKinley.

Just to the west of the Finger Lakes, the Genesee River flows down out of the Allegheny Plateau to Lake Ontario at Rochester. Because of obstructions in its former course, the Genesee has formed a new channel since the Ice Age. In doing so, a deep gorge has been eroded through great depths of sedimentary rocks. That spectacular gorge is the featured attraction of Letchworth State Park.

The Finger Lakes can be reached from Albany by way of Interstate 90, or Route 20, which is closer to the northern ends of the lakes. Route 20 continues westward to Letchworth State Park. Ithaca and Watkins Glen are located at the southern end of the two largest Finger Lakes.

Westward are Lake Erie at Buffalo and Niagara Falls, itself a product of the Ice Age. Water from Lake Erie spills over Niagara Falls and flows north through a gorge toward Lake Ontario. U.S. Route 104, the Robert Moses Parkway, follows the rim of the gorge north and eventually leads down a steep embankment onto another flat surface at a lower level. That embankment is the Niagara Escarpment, a cliff extending from the Niagara Gorge eastward to Rochester and westward beyond Lake Michigan. The escarpment is a fault line. As the glaciers melted away, a great weight was removed from the land. The rocks below were broken, and one side of the break rose above the other; water impounded south of the rock ledge became Lake Erie. Water of this new lake spilling over the escarpment formed the falls. Thus Niagara Falls began at the escarpment, 6½ miles north of its present location.

Gradually the river has worn a channel, cutting into the land to form a gorge. Even today the gorge is being lengthened as the falls retreat. The limestone at the rim of the falls is hard. Beneath the limestone, however, the rocks are quite soft and crumble rapidly. Water tumbling over the hard rim swirls about and cuts into the softer rocks at the bottom. Eventually those rocks are worn away, and the limestone at the top is left as a projecting ledge. Every few years another section of rock breaks away from the rim and tumbles into the depths below. Heaps of broken rock can be seen at the base of the falls. In such a way the falls continue to retreat southward and lengthen the gorge.

Much of the land bordering Lake Erie is quite flat, owing largely to the presence of brown clay. Wherever ditches are being dug or basements excavated, there is often much brown clay. On rainy days the clay becomes a very sticky mud. The clay that now covers the surface adjacent to Lake Erie came to the land as mud settling to the bottom of a much larger lake. The mud filled all of the low spots and was smoothed by gentle currents in the water, making the bottom of the lake a flat surface. Because the ice still covered Canada and blocked the Saint Lawrence Valley, the lake was deeper and wider than it is now. Lake Erie extended northward to the face of the ice and eastward into the Mohawk Valley as far as Little Falls. Lake Oneida is a remnant of that great glacial lake, as is Lake Erie itself.

At Little Falls the flat valley becomes narrow with cliffs of hard rock on each side. When Oneida was a vast glacial lake across the Mohawk Valley, the lake emptied through a spillway at Little Falls, like water over a dam. The lake is gone, but rapids remain. The hard black rocks that stand on each side of the rapids once extended all the way across the valley. The rapids are swift even today, but during the glacial times torrents of water spilled through the gorge from one cliff to the other. A volume of water even greater than that which spills over Niagara Falls cut an opening through the rock and formed the terrace where the city of Little Falls now stands. It is obvious that the Mohawk River of today is far smaller than the great river that drained the larger Great Lakes and shaped the valley across northern New York.

Glacial Evidence in the Midwest

The terminal moraine in the Midwest forms prominent hills but is not as massive as the moraines of Long Island and Cape Cod. No doubt the roughness of the terrain in the East resulted in an accumulation of more boulders, sand, and clay being scraped from the surface to be dumped in the moraine where the ice melted. Yet the diversion of streams on the western slopes of the Appalachians was perhaps greater than those of the highlands. For example, the Monongahela formerly flowed northward into the basin that is now Lake Erie, but with glacial ice and moraines obstructing the old course, a new channel to the south was developed. So today the Monongahela merges with the Allegheny at Pittsburgh to flow south and west as a new stream, the Ohio River. Other streams, likewise diverted, empty into the Ohio in its new course. One of these is the Scioto, which now flows south from Columbus, Ohio, emptying into the Ohio River at Portsmouth. Before ice covered the land, the Scioto flowed north into the Teays, a major stream that no longer exists, its northward channel completely filled and obliterated.

The terminal moraine in Ohio is marked by rolling hills extending from somewhat north of Pittsburgh southwestward to the southern outskirts of Columbus. From there the moraine continues in an irregular course toward southern Illinois. With drainage to the north no longer possible, the Ohio River developed a channel just beyond the moraine. But the moraine and the course of the Ohio often diverge locally. In developing its channel the new river followed the lowlands wherever possible. When this was impossible, the water was impounded and a lake formed. At one such point, waves on such a lake cut terraces into the surrounding hills. When the impounded waters cut through the obstruction, the water level of the lake was lowered and held there by harder rock at the outlet. At this lower level southwest winds produced waves, and the waves cut another terrace at the lower level in the surrounding hills. Thus a series of terraces were cut, and on these the small city of Portsmouth is now situated.

While the waters of the Ohio and surrounding areas south of the terminal moraine were impounded, outwash from the moraine filled the valleys of the Scioto and other lowlands. Now that water is flowing in the

Scioto again, much of the sediment that filled the valley has been removed, yet the old level of sediment is plainly evident as terraces along the sides of the valley, wider in some places than in others. Highways have been built on both sides of the Scioto Valley, following along the level terraces, dipping down occasionally where the modern meandering stream has cut away more of the terrace.

Glacier Activity in the West

With the continental glacier now gone from the East, we return to the West to see active glaciers, first in Glacier National Park, located close to the Canadian border in western Montana.

Glaciers on the sides of mountains in Glacier Park have broken away rocks and left jagged peaks in between. The glacial rocks washed into the valley below have formed a moraine that blocked the drainage and formed Saint Mary's Lake.

Glaciated regions have many lakes, formed when water drainage is blocked. Here at the edge of Silver Lake in the Cascades, vegetation is developing in the shallow water.

Highway 89 from Great Falls leads to the eastern entrance. There a single route, going to the Sun Road, crosses the park. Though once, in 1948, there were approximately 80 glaciers in the park, now there are closer to 50; the few visible from the highway are so small that they simply appear as patches of snow on the mountainsides. So in Glacier Park we must be content to enjoy the stupendous views of what glaciers have done to shape towering peaks, U-shaped valleys, and jagged ridges of rock. (Glaciers on mountainsides tend to break away the rocks in a kind of plucking action, carrying away dislodged stones.)

On entering the park from the east one soon comes to Saint Mary's Lake, located in a valley scoured out by glaciers. Streams from tributary valleys have emptied gravel at their mouths to block drainage and impound the waters of the lake. One such dam created by a tributary stream has divided the lake into two quite lengthy parts. Above the lake in plain sight are numerous jagged peaks of rock, created by glaciers. Some form ridges of hard rock, while others are pointed spires of rock, carved by glaciers on three sides. These are known as *horns,* the most noted being the Matterhorn of the Swiss Alps. Horns are numerous in Glacier Park. Reynolds Mountain at Logan Pass is one prominent example. Bearhat and Clements Mountains are two others visible from the pass. Logan Pass also provides a fine view of Saint Mary's Valley. Glaciers moving along the valley have rounded it out, cut back the sides, and converted sharp bends of a former river valley to the gentle curves of a typical glaciated valley.

As one descends from Logan Pass, the Garden Wall towers above on the left. Glaciers on both sides have narrowed the ridge. All that remains is a line of sharp-crested stone columns, called the *Garden Wall*. Geologists call such a narrow ridge of hard rock shaped by glaciers an *arête*. Admittedly there is much more to be seen in Glacier Park, but we have seen what is typical of glaciated mountains. Heading still farther west, Route 2 leads through scenic northern Idaho to Spokane, Washington. Continuing westward through the wide-open spaces of eastern Washington, Route 2 crosses the Cascades by way of Steven Pass. Either this pass or the Snoqualamie Pass on Route 90 will provide a good view of the mountains and their influence on the climate as previously described. Many alternative routes are possible.

In Glacier Park massive glaciers have moved along a previously narrow stream valley, gouging it out, rounding and widening it to form a U-shaped valley typical of glacial geology.

From near the Canadian border, the Mount Baker Highway, Route 542, runs eastward out of Bellingham, Washington. The highway ends on the slopes of Mount Baker. There the best glacier in sight is on Mount Shuksan, close by to the east. It is an ideal example of a hanging glacier—hanging because it ends at a precipice. As the ice advances, the end breaks off and tumbles down. A better view of the glaciers on Mount Baker itself can be obtained by returning a short way back down the highway to the Glacier Creek Road. Following that road a short distance to the south provides a more distant yet better view of the Colemen Glacier on Mount Baker. A short distance beyond the Coleman Glacier is Roosevelt Glacier.

The main entrance to Mount Rainier National Park is at the southwest corner by way of Route 7 from Tacoma. From the park headquarters and visitor's center the road inside the park climbs past the Nisqually Glacier to Paradise Inn. As has been noted, the Nisqually Glacier has been receding and is no longer in sight of the road. Glaciers advance when snowfall is heavy and recede when melting is predominant. The general trend of recession was reversed for a time during the 1960s. Apparently similar variations were characteristic of the continental glaciers during the Ice Age, as evidenced by the formation of recessional moraines, followed in some cases by advances in which the morainal material was overrun to form drumlins.

From the resort area at Paradise, short trails lead to observation points where glaciers on the mountain can be seen close at hand. The Stevens Canyon Road, which leads eastward from the Paradise Visitor Center, is open from mid-June to mid-October, whereas the Nisqually River entrance is open all year, weather permitting. Viewpoints along the Stevens Canyon Road provide fine views of the mountain and its glaciers. In addition, snowcapped Mount Adams is conspicuous to the south. Along this route, too, the headwaters of the Cowlitz River can be seen far below in the depths of a very narrow box canyon, which apparently is an eroded fault line.

The number of glaciers in the Olympic Mountains of northwest Washington has been estimated at about 50. The Blue Glacier, the Hoh, and a few others are quite large, but none of the glaciers here are accessible by road. Good roads do lead up into the mountains from Port Angeles to Hurricane Ridge. From there can be seen the snowcapped peaks, including the highest, Mount Olympus, from which the principal glaciers emanate. However, the big glaciers are on the opposite side, the west, facing the ocean from which come the moisture-laden winds.

Mount Hood, a dormant volcanic peak in Oregon, a short distance east of Portland, has conspicuous glaciers in sight of Highways 35 and 26, known as the Mount Hood Loop. Route 35 leads south from the Columbia River Drive, just west of the Dalles. The Loop Highway crosses the White River near that river's source at the White River Glacier. It should be noted that pulverized rock from the glacier has made the water white and gives the river its name.

For those who seek more spectacular views of active glaciers close to the highways, some fine examples are readily accessible a bit farther north in Canada. The Icefield Parkway on Route 93 from Banff National Park through the adjoining Jasper National Park is well named. There in British Columbia glaciers are abundant and readily visible from close range along the highway. The ice field section of Route 93 begins in the northern portion of Banff National Park and continues through most of Jasper National Park. A featured attraction is the Athabasca Glacier, which originates in an extensive upland, the Columbia Ice Field, with only the near edge of the great mass visible from the highway. The glacier descends over several ridges of rock, rounding out a broad valley and depositing glacial till along lateral moraines. Good-sized tributary glaciers among jagged peaks add to the view. The terminus, a short way from the highway, is readily accessible across an outwash plain. The Athabasca River begins here and on its way to the Arctic can be seen along the highway farther north.

More live glaciers can be viewed by taking a cruise ship out of Seattle along the inland waterway of southern Alaska. A trip on the Alaska Railroad to Mount McKinley will reveal many spectacular scenes, including huge glaciers on the side of the tallest mountain in North America.

6

PLAINS AND PLATEAUS

In an art class, a boy from the West Coast attending the campus school of an eastern university was directed to make a sketch of mountains. He did so, drawing the sharply jagged, saw-toothed outline commonly used in the West to represent mountain peaks. The art teacher, carefully supervising, saw what the boy was doing, and gently corrected him, demonstrating how mountains should be represented by softly rounded curves.

Sharply pointed peaks are common in the West, but not in the East, where mountains have become quite worn and rounded, an appearance familiar to the eastern art instructor. The Appalachians have a long history of erosion. Streams have cut back the surface so that rounded forms are predominant. In contrast the mountains of the West are younger, with volcanic peaks and glaciated mountains made jagged by the glaciers on their flanks.

Wherever mountains are high, rain and snow are likely to be heavy. Where the snow becomes compacted to form ice, glaciers cut into the mountainside, and meltwater carries away loose rocks. Rocks crumble in this destructive weather, and boulders break away at their joints. Gradually but persistently, vast amounts of rock flour are removed and carried away in swift streams flowing down the mountainside. Upon reaching the lowland, the streams are no longer so swift; so the sediment settles out, coarse rocks first, followed by finer particles. In this way, the lowland is gradually built up as the mountains are cut down. In the West as the Rocky Mountains continue to be uplifted, more and more sediment is carried down onto the Great Plains.

The Great Plains

Three rivers off the eastern slopes of the Rocky Mountains in Montana merge to form the Missouri River, which flows down out of the mountains onto the Great Plains. Along its course it is joined by several more streams

A view of Denver, Colorado, with the Front Range of the Rocky Mountains beyond. Denver is on the High Plains at the foot of the Rockies. The Front Range was elevated along a major fault line.

out of the mountains. The Yellowstone River flows out of the mountains in Wyoming and empties into the Missouri. As the Missouri crosses the Dakotas, the Little Missouri River, the Big Muddy, the Grand River, Cheyenne River, and a number of smaller streams empty into the Missouri, each bringing with it a load of mud out of the mountains. Such streams are commonly brown with the mud they carry. Is there any wonder that the Missouri is often spoken of as the "Big Muddy"? In Nebraska the Nebraska and the Platte Rivers with all their branches add more sediment from the southern Rocky Mountains. In Kansas a network of other rivers add their loads. Still farther south, the Arkansas River also drains the southern Rockies, as do the Pecos River and the Rio Grande.

Much of the sediment from the Rocky Mountains is carried into the Mississippi River, which empties it into the Gulf of Mexico, building a growing delta there. The city of New Orleans stands on that delta, on land brought down from the mountains. Yet not all of the sediment from the mountains reaches the Gulf of Mexico. After every flood, citizens who live along the rivers can testify that much of the mud is spread across fields, enriching the farmland. After the flood recedes, homeowners have to clean up the mud. A new layer of mud, a stratum of sediment, is also added to the floodplain of the river. Navigable rivers often have to be dredged to keep their channels open and to reduce the hazards of further floods. Lakes and reservoirs gradually fill with sediment and become too shallow to provide the water needed for irrigation, or to turn the generators that produce electricity at power dams.

Although farmers' fields may be enriched by fresh sediment, the mud can be problematic for farmers. Homes and factories built conveniently close to riverbanks on the good flat land of a floodplain can be severely damaged by water and mud during unexpected floods. Unfortunately, it is often overlooked that the land beside a stream is flat because it is a floodplain and does flood every once in a while. The sediment carried out over the land in a flood settles rather uniformly onto the land, filling low areas and developing the smooth surface of a floodplain.

The Great Plains have been built by the repeated flooding of muddy streams out of the Rocky Mountains. The Great Plains close to the mountains have also been uplifted as the adjoining mountains were pressed upward. Denver, for example, often is spoken of as if it were in the Rocky Mountains. Actually, the Mile High City is on the Great Plains at the foot of the southern Rockies, even though truly a mile high.

With good reason, the Great Plains close to the mountains are termed the "high plains." They are in fact high enough to be subject to erosion. In the south, the Red River drains those high plains, flowing southeast to the Mississippi River and the Gulf of Mexico. At times the river is appropriately named, running red with the rusty sediment it carries. With other streams likewise cutting into the high plains, they are in some places being cut to pieces. The Badlands of South Dakota are an extreme example of this process. The Little Missouri in North Dakota provides another example. Even though the High Plains are on the leeward side of the mountain range and rainfall is light, streams coming down out of the mountains do cut into the High Plains, removing sediment deposited in the past and creating badlandslike landscapes.

In the East, from the Mohawk Valley south into Alabama, the plateaus of the Appalachians have been similarly constructed, built of sediment washed off the once-tall Appalachian Mountains. Though erosion is often more extreme in some parts than others, significant erosion has occurred throughout the Appalachian Plateau and continues today. Southeastern

Although on the leeward side of the mountains and quite dry, the Great Plains of South Dakota have been severely eroded by streams out of the mountains, forming the "Badlands."

Ohio is a portion of the plateau surface already dissected into rounded or flat-topped hills. The original plateau surface is still evident in the uniform height of the hills derived from the original plateau. In the Allegheny Plateau, the Allegheny River flows south to Pittsburgh where it merges with the Monongahela out of West Virginia and becomes the Ohio River. Over the years the regions alongside the Ohio have been plagued with some spectacular floods. The water levels of the 1889 Johnstown flood are still marked on civic buildings of the city. The Ohio itself and other tributaries have had severe floods, and though flood walls along the banks now reduce the hazards, they cannot eliminate them. Significantly, the streams are still cutting into the highlands, carrying away sediment, deepening the valleys, and leaving behind the rounded or flat-topped hills of uniform height where the plateau surface once was. Farther south, the Cumberland and Tennessee Rivers are cutting into the Cumberland Plateau.

In the Ozark Plateau the process is similar. Originally a comparatively uniform surface, the plateau now is being cut by erosion, so that many of the roads in the area now ride like roller coasters.

The Appalachian Plateaus

From Albany, New York, on a clear day, the flat tops of the Catskills can be seen outlined against the sky. They stand well above the surrounding Allegheny Plateau. Deep notches have been eroded into the flat surfaces of the Catskill Mountains. At one time these surfaces were much wider than they are today, for continuing erosion has carried away a large portion of the upper surface. The floods on Schoharie Creek at Gilboa, where the fossil trees were exposed, provide evidence that erosion is still changing the Catskills.

Entering the Catskills from the Hudson Valley, Route 23A ascends through a deep gorge that has been cut into the high plateau. Along the

The coarse red sandstone of the Catskills, the delta of a great river running out of ancient New England mountains into the New York lowland. The Hudson Valley now separates the delta from the mountains.

Here in the Catskills are the fossil stumps of ancient trees in the oldest forest known. These tree ferns, now found only in the tropics, grew on the shore of a Devonian inland sea at the edge of the Catskill Delta, about 300 million years ago.

sides of the gorge sit the rocks of which the Catskills are made. At the top is a thick layer of red sandstone. The sandstone consists of sand washed down out of mountains farther east. When the sand was deposited here, the land was low, a broad surface sloping gently westward. The mountains of New England then were high and rugged. A great river spilled out of the New England mountains into the lowlands of this vicinity. Upon reaching the lowland, the swift current spread and became a broad, muddy delta. Gravel and boulders were left upstream on the slopes of the mountains. With each heavy rain in the mountains, more sand washed down into the lowlands and was deposited there. The mud remained in the water and was deposited farther west.

On the surface of the Catskill Plateau it is evident that modern streams are cutting into the sandstone surface so that the plateau is no longer as broad and flat as it appeared from a distance. The soil is red and sandy, for the sandstone is gradually crumbling.

Cornell University is located on the Allegheny Plateau overlooking the glacial Cayuga Lake and the city of Ithaca. Fall Creek runs through the university campus grounds, on the surface of the broad plateau. At the edge of the campus the water of the creek pitches abruptly down over a waterfall and flows through a narrow gorge. The stream plunges over a series of cascades through increasingly deep gorges until at last the creek broadens and flows quietly through the city, across a lowland and into Cayuga Lake. The increasingly deep channel of the creek reveals to some extent what lies below the surface of the plateau and suggests how deep

At Watkins Glen, New York, a small stream has cut a gorge into the sandstone of the Catskill Delta. The sandstone farther from the mountains is finer and gray in color, having been deposited under water with little oxygen available to form rust.

the sediments are and how great was the volume of sediment that was washed off the ancient mountains of New England. On each side of the gorge cut by the creek is fine gray sandstone in thin layers as deep as can be seen. What is visible is but a tiny portion of what lies below the university campus and the adjoining farmlands. The entire plateau is made of fine sand in layers of sandstone, the sand carried here long ago by streams from the east.

From Ithaca, at the end of Cayuga Lake, 20 miles west is Watkins Glen, located at the end of Seneca Lake, another glacial lake. Here an even greater gorge has been cut into the same fine gray sandstone. A trail follows the stream that cut into the plateau and exposed the fine sandstone. At one point sheets of water plunge over a sparkling waterfall. Above the stream on the rocky walls are many rounded, hollow forms, shaped by the swirling current before the stream had cut to its present depth.

A salt refinery can be seen in the distance at the southern end of Seneca Lake in New York. The lake is deep, with salt beds on the lake floor formed as the inland sea evaporated.

PLAINS AND PLATEAUS

The layers of sediment extend over a broad area across the state to the western border and beyond. It is hard to comprehend that such vast amounts of sand could have been carried here by streams out of New England mountains. Yet modern streams, such as the Mississippi, are today spreading similarly vast amounts of sediment. The Mississippi Delta at New Orleans extends far out into the gulf, most of it covered by water. As more and more sediment is added, mud settles to the bottom and a fan-shaped deposit is built farther out into the water.

The Catskill Delta was built in the same way. A great river flowed out of the mountains somewhere near Albany and spread from there out across the lowland. Other streams to the north and south likewise carried sediment into the flats. The deposits of sand and clay grew deeper and farther into the lowland with each passing century. Now that the rugged mountains and the rivers are gone, the sand and clay remain in the plateau to reveal what happened.

Far beyond Watkins Glen, across the uneven, eroded surface of the plateau, is Letchworth State Park. There the Genesee River has cut a tremendous gorge into the plateau, plunging over a series of waterfalls, cutting ever deeper into the sediments of the plateau, then flowing northward toward Rochester and Lake Ontario. The flat surface of the plateau is plainly evident above the gorge. The level land on each side is wooded. Observation points along the rim of the gorge provide fascinating views of the river far below. The walls of the gorge are marked by horizontal lines of sedimentary rock, the same formations seen at Watkins Glen and Ithaca. The sandstone of the Catskills is red and coarse. Farther west the sand particles are fine and gray. At Letchworth there is some fine sandstone, but most layers of rock are shale in various shades of gray and black.

In the Catskills the sandstone is red because of iron rust in the sand. Iron weathered from the rocks of the mountains was deposited with the sand. The iron in the moist beds of sand oxidized, and the rust acted as a cement, changing loose sand into sandstone. Finer grains of sand were carried out across the delta to an inland sea. These coalesced into the fine-grained sandstone observed at Ithaca and Watkins Glen. But there the sand was under water, with little free oxygen for the rusting process, and so the sandstone became gray instead. Only the very fine particles of sand and clay were carried far into the sea, where Letchworth Park is now located.

At Letchworth State Park the Genesee River has cut a deep gorge in the sediments of the Allegheny Plateau. Visible here are many layers of sediment and a resistant stratum at the waterfall.

Still farther west, beyond Buffalo, is Niagara Falls. A visitor standing beside the falls at Prospect Point can see the river, divided near the center by Goat Island, flowing smoothly toward the rim of the falls, then dropping abruptly into the gorge. A swirling cloud rises from the tumbling water, and gasps of amazement are lost in the roar of plunging water. The rim of Niagara Falls is a kind of limestone called dolomite. Below the rim are layers of shale, sandstone, and more limestone. From the falls the various layers of rock extend south and east into the Allegheny Plateau, beneath the sediments of the Catskill Delta. Because the Niagara formations sit below those of the delta, we know they are older.

In fact, the Catskill Delta was formed in the Devonian Period. The Niagara limestone and other sediments were deposited in the preceding period, the Silurian. The Silurian and Devonian Periods occurred near the middle of the Paleozoic Era. Throughout the Paleozoic there were mountains in the east, but the Folded Appalachians and the adjoining plateaus had not yet been thrust upward.

The layers of rock at Niagara Falls can be seen extending northward along the sides of the gorge. The same formations are plainly evident in a bluff beside the highway that runs along the shore of Lake Ontario eastward to Rochester. The limestone, shale, and sandstone also can be traced southward along the banks of the Genesee gorge and eastward at the edge of the Mohawk Valley. Silurian rocks then extend throughout the plateau, across the state from Niagara Falls and Lake Ontario to the Hudson Valley.

The same Silurian rocks are found in Shawangunk Mountain, a low ridge of sandstone and conglomerate that has hardened to become

Niagara Falls: Dislodged rocks at the base of the falls are visible on the right through the mist. The hard rocks at the rim of the falls tumble down as softer rocks below are cut away by the swirling water; thus the falls gradually retreat upstream.

quartzite. The ridge begins near Rosendale, New York (near the Hudson River, south of Kingston), and extends southwestward into Pennsylvania. Across the Pennsylvania line this mountainous ridge is known as Kittatiny Mountain. Kittatiny is at the base of the Poconos, where the Delaware River has cut a water gap. Still farther south the same ridge is known as Blue Mountain.

Near Rosendale the particles in the ridge are gravel-size, forming conglomerate rather than sandstone. These coarse sediments indicate that a swift river flowed out of eastern mountains at this point. The sediments were spread out across a lowland in all directions, out across New York and Pennsylvania, as far as Niagara Falls and beyond. Those sediments represent another delta, similar to the Catskill Delta but older.

As with the Catskill Delta, the coarse gravel and sand were deposited at the foot of the eastern mountains. Finer sediments were carried farther west. Beyond the Niagara gorge the sediments were predominantly mud,

Niagara Gorge beyond the falls. The dolomite limestone at the top here is the hard rock that forms the rim of the falls. As the falls retreat, the gorge is lengthened, and the strata below the plateau are exposed.

Shawangunk Mountain in southeastern New York, formed of sandstone and conglomerate from a Silurian Delta out of New England mountains, and older than the Devonian Catskill Delta, with sediments beneath those of the Catskills throughout the plateau.

now shale. Still farther west in Ontario, Canada, the rocks are almost all limestone, indicating that lime settled to the bottom of an inland sea that covered the region.

As time went by, the sea covering New York shrank, much in the same way as what is taking place now in the West at Salt Lake. Great Salt Lake in Utah is all that remains of a far larger lake that once covered much of Utah and Nevada. As the lake has become smaller, the water has become more and more salty. Beyond the south and west edges of the present lake all the water is gone; nothing remains but deep beds of salt. And the process is continuing as the lake loses water to evaporation more rapidly than it gains fresh water from the few small streams that supply it. Some day there may be nothing left but vast white beds of salt.

In much the same way, an even greater sea once covered most of New York and parts of the neighboring states. The water gradually evaporated, with nothing left but the salt from the water. The salt beds of New York are no longer on the surface, for the sediments of the Allegheny Plateau have covered them.

In central New York, the salt deposits are more than 1,000 feet thick. At Ithaca the salt is about half a mile below the surface, covered by newer sediment. At Watkins Glen, two salt refineries are located on the edge of Seneca Lake. There is little to be seen at the surface, except the refinery buildings. The salt is so far below the bottom of the lake that the lake water is free of salt. Holes have been drilled down to the salt beds; water from the lake is pumped into the ground under great pressure. After becoming saturated with salt, the water is forced to the surface through drill holes and conducted in pipes to the refinery. There the brine is purified and evaporated to get the salt.

A short way north of Letchworth Park, south of Rochester, is a small town by the name of Retsof. There salt is mined from the ground much like coal. The Retsof mine is the largest of its kind in the Western Hemisphere. Since 1885, men have carved a network of underground rooms and tunnels out of the salt, about one-fifth of a mile below the surface.

Early settlers along the Mohawk Valley found springs seeping from the ground at Onondaga, near Syracuse. The water of the springs was saturated with salt. For a long time the brine from those springs was evaporated to obtain salt, the first commercial salt in America.

Long ago, after the beds of salt had formed, conditions again changed. Mountains once more were uplifted in the New England region. With abundant water again flowing into the lowlands, layers of sand and clay were deposited above the salt beds, forming the Catskill Delta above the old Silurian Sea. The vast salt beds and the great expanse of the Catskill Delta reveal what became of the massive eastern mountains that preceded the Appalachians.

At one point the Allegheny Plateau extended north to the Adirondack Mountains, but the Mohawk River has cut into the soft rocks of the plateau and formed a broad valley. Most of the cutting was done during the Ice Age while the current was swift, draining the Great Lakes while the St. Lawrence Valley was still blocked with ice. From Albany the Taconic Mountains of today can be seen beyond the Hudson Valley, near the New York–Massachusetts border. It is sometimes said that the Taconics are mountains without roots, which means they were not lifted up from below but were thrust out over older rocks by pressures from the east. At Albany the thrust fault along which the mountains were shoved inland is only about two or three miles east of the Hudson River, but erosion has cut back the face of the mountains a greater distance.

From Lexington, Kentucky, the Mountain Parkway leads southeast to Kentucky's Natural Bridge State Park. Although not widely known, the Natural Bridge is fascinating in terms of the geological processes it reveals. If we compare the level of the bridge with the uniform height of distant ridges, we can infer that once this was the surface of the land, the worn-down Appalachians. The surface of the bridge is a strong layer of conglomerate. It seems that gullies developed on each side of what now is the bridge. The result was a ridge with the conglomerate as a cap rock at the top. Then caves developed on each side in a stratum of less resistant rock. The caves deepened until they met beneath the bridge thus formed. A gully beneath the bridge extends down the hill to the parking lot of the park.

Since the surface of the bridge is the worn-down level of the original mountains, the distance down to the highway and the parking lot reveals the extent of erosion since the mountains were elevated to their present height. Concurrent with that uplift and erosion of the region, the stratum of conglomerate was undercut to form the bridge. With so much erosion, just since the reelevation of the worn surface, there was no lack of sediment to build the vast Appalachian Plateaus.

In the eastern portion of West Virginia, north of Bluefield, is Pinnacles State Park, in which an upended stratum of hard sandstone, shaped by erosion, provides a graphic example of the forces that built the Allegheny Mountains. Bordering these mountains on the west is the plateau, built of eroded sediments from the mountains.

Farther south the Blue Ridge and Piedmont ranges merge to form the Great Smoky Mountains, preserved as a national park. The Appalachian Trail is 2,000 miles long—a footpath from Mount Katahdin in northern Maine extending along the crest of the range south to the Blue Ridge and the Great Smoky Mountains of the southern Appalachians and Springer Mountain in Georgia. The crest of the Great Smokies marks the border between North Carolina and Tennessee. The mountaintops are clothed with a green forest of spruce, fir, birch, and mountain ash—trees similar to those at lower levels farther north. Because of their height, the Smokies have a cool climate. Warm southern air rising on the flanks of the mountains is cooled sufficiently to produce a blue haze that has the appearance of fog or smoke, hence the name.

Bordering the Smoky Mountains on the east is the Atlantic Coastal Plain. On the west is the Great Valley, eroded stumps of the Folded Appalachians and the Cumberland Mountains, a further portion of the Folded Appalachians, which like the Allegheny Mountains farther north are the upended strata that remain from the worn-down Appalachians. In contrast, the Cumberland Plateau close by on the west is composed of horizontal strata, sediments washed off the former Appalachians. The mountains here are a great mass of hard conglomerate rock thrust up over shale along a great fault line plainly visible at Pine Mountain, about 85 miles north across the border in Kentucky. The coarse rock on the mountaintops and the hard sandstone that forms the upper surface of the adjoining plateau indicate that the stones and sand came from swift streams flowing west off tall mountains in the east. Thus once again we

Figure 62 Seashells in the limestone of the Shenandoah Valley indicate the rock was formed from lime in a shallow sea before the Appalachians were elevated, about a half million years ago.

The Cumberland Plateau in northern Alabama consists of horizontal sediments, strata from once lofty Appalachian Mountains. A small stream has cut a gorge and exposed the uplifted sediments.

see that the erosion that cut down the tall Appalachians provided the sediments that built the plateaus.

Long before the Cumberland Plateau was uplifted, a shallow sea occupied a vast area of what is now Kentucky, Tennessee, and neighboring states. Lime settled from the quiet water, forming limestone deposits on the bottom of the sea. The lime formed slowly; yet over a great expanse of time, the mass of rock on the bottom became as much as one-quarter of a mile deep, in some places even deeper.

After the plateau was uplifted, erosion began. Water washed down out of the mountains, carrying with it bits of decaying vegetation. (One product of decay is carbon dioxide. In water carbon dioxide becomes carbonic acid, a weak acid, but one nevertheless able to dissolve limestone.) The water that seeped through the "sour" soil became slightly acidic. Wherever such water soaked into cracks between blocks of limestone, some of the rock dissolved, and the openings became larger. Eventually the openings became caverns, a great series of underground rooms.

A wind gap in the Blue Ridge (center of the picture), worn by a stream flowing to the Atlantic at the level of the ridge. Erosion of the valley in the foreground has diverted the stream, now crossed by the highway bridge in the valley.

The basin in which Nashville, Tennessee, is located has been eroded from the higher ground of the plateau with the help of the Cumberland River, which still flows through Nashville from higher ground to the east. In Kentucky this eroded plateau gradually becomes a limestone region with numerous caverns, among them Mammoth Cave, perhaps the most noted. Sinkholes and underground streams are common, and limestone in the soil gives the Bluegrass region a distinctive quality. Other limestone regions are extensive throughout the Midwest and West, such as Indiana limestone and the Carlsbad Caverns of New Mexico. As limestone is derived from calm, deep water, it is clear that much of the inland region was covered by deep water for a long period of time, located far from the mountains, beyond their eroded sand and clay.

The Tennessee River begins in the Cumberland Plateau, flows south into Alabama, then curves north across Tennessee into the Ohio River, thence to the Mississippi and the Gulf of Mexico. Thus in this instance, as in many others, the eroded sediments of the Appalachians are transported to the Gulf of Mexico rather than to the nearby Atlantic, preserving the limestone formations.

Sediments of the Coastal Plain

The sands of the Atlantic Coastal Plain accumulated over a long expanse of time while lofty mountains were being cut down. Even today eastward-flowing streams empty their sediments at the shore. During storms pounding waves add to the debris. Beyond the beaches much of the sediment is covered by the shallow waters of the continental shelf, with still more washed farther out into the depths of the Atlantic. In the north, the rockbound coast of Maine has few sandy beaches. There the sediments spread into the Gulf of Maine are largely covered by shallow water of the banks where commercial fishing thrives.

Farther south, by the Piedmont range, a sandy coastal plain stands between the hard rocks of the worn-down mountains and the shore. The sands of the coastal plain are shallow close to the inner edge but deeper toward the shore, and deeper still farther offshore. Beneath those sands of the coastal plain are more hard rocks from the base of once-tall mountains, and those hard rocks continue beneath the sands to the edge of the continental shelf. Beyond the steep slope of the shelf, the continent ends abruptly, where the continent of Africa once stood. Since Africa drifted away, opening up the Atlantic, sediments from the eroding mountains have been washed into the void.

Where streams flow across the hard rocks of the Piedmont onto the less resistant coastal sediments, rapids have developed. As a consequence the point at which the Piedmont rocks end at the coastal plain has become known as the Fall Line.

Chesapeake Bay is a broad inland waterway that has many stubby branches. The flat coastal lands surrounding the bay have gone through numerous changes. Seashells found there indicate that the land was under water for a time. The flat surface of the terraces suggest they have been smoothed by ocean waves that formerly swept over them. Yet during the Ice Age, the sea level was lower and the shoreline farther east than it is today. The fossil bones and teeth of Ice Age elephants have been dredged from the sediments in shallow water beyond the shore, indicating that these animals roamed there when it was dry land. In those days the York and James Rivers emptied into the Susquehanna and flowed with it eastward into the ocean. The Potomac, the Rappahannock, and others likewise merged with the Susquehanna. The merging streams cut valleys that came together like the branches of a tree.

Several thousand years ago, when the Ice Age ended and the ice melted, the sea level rose and the trunk of that branching tree flooded, forming what is now Chesapeake Bay. Even some of the branches are flooded, so that much of the Potomac, the York, and the James are more like bays than like rivers.

The battle that ended the American Revolution was fought on a terrace above the York River. One of the entrenched positions of the British, known as Redoubt Number Ten, is close to the bluff. In subsequent years the fortifications preserved as a memorial park have been partially destroyed. With each storm on Chesapeake Bay, waves have cut into the foot of the cliff. The weak sandstone has been worn away, with the sand spreading along a narrow beach at the foot of the cliff. In some places the upper portion of the bluff overhangs a cavity at beach level, undercut by the waves. Occasionally some of the upper portion will tumble down, and the face of the bluff is changed. To a large extent, the position won in battle has been lost to the river through erosion of the bank.

The Great Dismal Swamp farther south is on a flat surface somewhat similar to the Yorktown terraces but at a lower elevation. The swamp is located on the Virginia–North Carolina border not far from shore. Water has gathered in the low areas, and cypress trees now stand above the shallow water. A good view of the swamp can be obtained from U.S. Highway 158, just east of Elizabeth City, North Carolina, on the way from Jamestown to Kitty Hawk, located on a barrier beach.

From Norfolk, Virginia, a ridge of sand, sometimes wide and sometimes narrow, stands between the land and the open sea. Ocean waves toss the sand toward the shore, especially during violent storms. The sand never quite reaches the shore though and instead forms what is generally known as the Outer Banks but what geologists term *barrier beaches,* or sometimes *barrier islands.*

Atlantic City is built on a barrier beach, and so is Miami Beach, though of course not all barrier beaches are as massive as these. Construction on a barrier beach is hazardous, because the foundation is simply a ridge of sand and can be damaged during a severe storm. In recent years the problems encountered on the barrier beach at Cape Hatteras, North Carolina, demonstrate what can happen. When ocean waves encounter shallow water, the underwater base of the wave is held back, and as when a runner is tripped, the crest of the wave pitches forward. Such breakers can strike the shore with tremendous force and do severe damage. Beaches can be ideal campgrounds but are generally not safe for permanent structures. Between a barrier beach and the shore is a body of shallow water termed a lagoon. If the barrier beach is not destroyed during a storm, sediment will accumulate in the lagoon until saltwater plants begin to grow in the ever more shallow water, and the lagoon becomes marshland.

Ocean currents and incoming waves, aided by strong winds, spread sand along the shore in the direction of breaking waves. The sand may form a sandbar across an embayment, or if the waves strike at an angle, the result may be a ridge of sand projecting from the land into shallow water, forming a spit, often curving at the end, like the northern tip of Cape Cod.

Along the California coast, where the land is rising, areas of flat land, terraces, stand close to a bluff above the water. It is evident there that waves have cut into the coast, reducing the land to sea level, but the worn surface since has been uplifted to form a terrace well above the waves. In general the Atlantic coast is no longer rising, but there are a few places where wave-cut terraces are found along the rocky coast of Maine. It seems the land there has risen somewhat since the weight of once-massive glaciers has been removed.

Scientists from Cornell University have reported the detection of a deep fault extending diagonally across the coastal plain of Georgia. The fault runs northward out to sea and southward to the Gulf of Mexico, which may explain the emergence of Florida from the sea subsequent to the rise of the Appalachians. Magnetic anomalies and similarities of crustal forma-tions in Florida with those of the African coast suggest that Florida was a portion of Africa that remained attached to the North American continent. It is possible that with the removal of continental pressure the landmass of Florida rose to the surface. The uplift was somewhat uneven, and the Okefenokee Swamp in Georgia near the Florida line remains low today. The Everglades in the south and Lake Okeechobee are also portions of an uneven surface only slightly above sea level. A large portion of Florida consists of limestone, much of it containing seashells, revealing the comparatively recent elevation of the land.

The limestone of Florida provides some rich land for citrus groves but is not without its problems. When slightly acidic water created from vegetation decaying at the surface seeps into beds of limestone, it dissolves the lime, forming underground caverns. If the cavity holds water, a pond may be formed. But if the cavity collapses into a sinkhole, possibly swallowing a home, factory, or segment of highway, the damage can be serious.

The Gulf Coastal Plain is built of sediments brought down by the Mississippi River out of the Rocky Mountains and also the Appalachians. At one time the Gulf of Mexico extended into northern Alabama. Stream-rounded pebbles can be found where streams once emptied directly into the gulf. Sand was carried farther out into the water, making a stratum of sand, which today is known as Tuscaloosa sandstone, after the university town where the sandstone is plainly visible. In still deeper water, fine particles of clay and lime settled out of the water, along with tiny bits of sand, forming a mixture known as marl. In central Alabama that mixture, rich in lime, has made very good farmland, the soil dark with humus (decayed vegetation). Because of the dark soil stretching across the state from east to west, it is called the Black Belt. Thus the coastal plain across the South often is spoken of as the "Belted Plains," with the characteristics of each belt depending upon the strata of sediment exposed there. In one belt, easily eroded clay has been reduced to rather flat land now covered with trees. Hence that belt is known as the Flatwoods. Adjoining it is a belt of more resistant sandstone, partially eroded to form hills, now termed the Red Hills, because of the rusty iron that served as a cement in the sandstone. Another is quite level and known as the Dougherty Plain. Still another belt of sediment supports a pine forest, the Southern Pine Hills.

Like the Atlantic Coastal Plain, the Southern Plains stand on a base of hard rock, which in this case may represent a continuation of the worn-down Appalachians, depressed to form a slope toward the Gulf of Mexico. Along the northern edge of the Gulf Coastal Plain, where the sedimentary deposits stand higher, erosion has cut the surface into hills, corresponding to the erosion of the High Plains close to the Rocky Mountains.

West of the Mississippi lowland, the coastal plain from the Ouachita Mountains south to the gulf consists of belts somewhat similar to those of Alabama. In one area especially the similarity is remarkable, with the presence of a black belt, also due to soil rich with lime and humus. In that western portion of the Gulf Coastal Plain, erosion is continued by the Brazos, Trinity, and other rivers carrying away sediment. Along the inner portion of this western coastal plain, many small rounded pebbles are conspicuous in the soil, suggesting they came from streams eroding the nearby Ouachita Mountains.

The Mississippi lowland is a depressed area that has accumulated sediments from mountains both east and west, forming an embayment, a northward extension of the coastal plain. The region is commonly spoken of as the "delta" area, because of the flat land built of sediments from the river. The Mississippi Valley is uniformly low. It is noteworthy that the highest point in Louisiana, Driskill Mountain, is only 535 feet high—yet still called a mountain!

7

ROCKS, FOSSILS, AND MOUNTAINS

Rocks are divided into three categories: igneous rocks, which are formed when magma flows up from deeper regions in the earth's crust and hardens; sedimentary rocks, which are formed when layers of sediment are compacted together; and metamorphic rocks, which are formed when any type of rock is altered by heat, pressure, shearing, or chemical processes, to create a new type of rock.

Igneous Rocks

Most people are somewhat familiar with *granite,* a common type of rock used for tombstones and monuments. Granite is found in mountainous regions or where mountains once were, such as the Piedmont. Granite is an igneous rock, which means it has come directly from deep within the earth as molten rock. Other kinds of igneous rocks include lavas that have cooled and hardened before reaching the surface.

All rocks consist of minerals. The mineral content of rocks varies, but minerals are definite chemical compounds, or at least closely related compounds. Granite consists of quartz, feldspar, and a dark mineral such as mica or hornblende. Most granite is predominantly white with only a speckling of dark minerals. Some granite has a slightly pink or salmon-red appearance, due to the presence of feldspar (though other feldspars are white). Though little known, feldspar is the most common of all minerals. When exposed to the elements, however, feldspar gradually crumbles to form clay, and when wet, the familiar mud. When the feldspar in granite crumbles, crystals of quartz are washed away as sand. Almost all grains of sand are bits of quartz. There are exceptions, though, such as the black sands of beaches in Hawaii. There volcanic basalt pounded by waves has broken into grains of black sand. Granite is a resistant rock, but when it does crumble, bits of the dark minerals may be seen in the clay or sand, if the tiny particles have not been washed away in the rain.

Rocks similar to granite but with greater amounts of the dark minerals are called *gabbros*. Inasmuch as the difference between a gabbro and a granite is based upon the types of minerals, the distinction may not be easy to make by casual examination. Hence coarse rocks like granite but of uncertain composition are simply called *granitoid* rocks.

Granitoid rocks have large crystals, a result of slow cooling in the depths of mountains, allowing time for crystals to grow. Erosion is

The granite in this quarry was formed as molten rock rose and hardened deep within the Green Mountains of Vermont. The mountains above have since been worn away.

The stone on the left is *granite*. The one on the right is *gabbro*. Both are igneous, formed as magma rises and hardens beneath the crust. The white mineral in granite is feldspar; what appears as gray is actually a glassy quartz. Gabbro has more dark minerals in place of quartz.

generally responsible for bringing granitoid rocks to the surface. If the molten rock cooled quickly at or near the surface, the crystals would be smaller. Rocks of light color like granite but with tiny crystals, scarcely perceptible without magnification, are termed *felsites*. If the dark minerals are predominant, as in gabbro, but the crystal grains are quite small, the rock is *basalt,* a rock found most often where there have been effusive lava flows.

Besides the less common felsite and gabbro (a granitoid rock), there are other terms used by mineralogists to describe igneous rocks based on mineral content and crystal size. Pegmatite is simply a granite with extremely large crystals. Pegmatite mines are a good source of large crystals for special purposes, for example, to provide an alternative to impure clays in the production of such ceramics as fine china. Obsidian represents the opposite extreme. It is a volcanic glass with minerals like

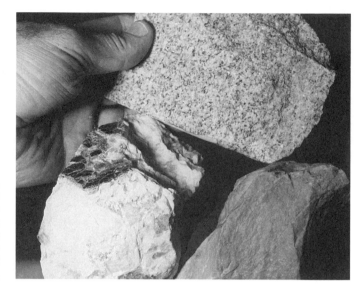

Here are granite (top), pegmatite (left), and a felsite (right). All of these contain the same minerals, but have crystals of different sizes. Igneous rocks are named according to their mineral content and the size of their crystals.

those of granite but with no crystals at all. It may seem that obsidian consists largely of dark minerals, unlike granite, but the dark minerals here are so small and uniformly dispersed that they make the glasslike lava seem black.

Each kind of mineral has a distinctive form of crystal. At the top from the left is *mica*, *asbestos*, and a dark red *garnet*. At the front left is *quartz* (silica), *calcite* (lime), *halite* (salt), *feldspar* (which weathers to form clay), and *iron pyrite* (fool's gold).

Sedimentary Rocks

Common sedimentary rocks are much more familiar than most igneous rocks. *Sandstone* is simply "cemented" sand, with the sandstone only as strong as the glue that holds it together. A common cement is simply iron rust, giving the rock a dull red color, but the bond is weak. If the cement is quartz, as is the sand itself, the rock will be hard and strong. *Conglomerate* is formed in much the same way as sandstone but with rounded pebbles instead of sand. It often contains sand as well, which furthers the similarity to sandstone. Here too the rock can be hard and erosion resistant if the cement is strong. Conglomerate is much like concrete and on occasion can be mistaken for it. Concrete is made of sand and gravel, held together by limestone and shale, in a sense an artificial conglomerate.

Shale is hardened, compacted clay, generally from river deltas or lake and ocean bottoms. It is the most abundant of all sedimentary rocks. *Limestone* is simply lime that has precipitated out of water. It is white in color, but "impurities" commonly make it somewhat gray. *Chert* is impure quartz that like lime has precipitated out of water. It is not especially common, except in certain areas such as the Ozarks and other areas close to the Mississippi Valley. Whatever color the rock may have depends on any other minerals that are in it. Chert is found most commonly in limestone regions, inasmuch as both are deposited from water.

Loess is not a rock but windblown dust, mostly clay. In the Midwest during the Ice Age, with water locked up in glaciers, the land became very dry, and great depths of windblown sediment, loess, are found in many localities there. *Marl* is a mixture of clay with lime, sometimes containing seashells. It is most often found in the southern coastal plains. *Silt* is merely fine rock particles from a stream bed. *Humus* is soil containing decayed vegetation; it serves as an excellent fertilizer. *Loam* refers to soil that is a mixture of sand and clay. It may be a sandy loam or a clay loam, depending on which is predominant. Of the sedimentary rocks, the most common are sandstone, shale, and limestone, with conglomerate and chert less common. Conglomerate, nevertheless, is significant in indicating where streams once flowed.

Metamorphic Rocks

Gneiss (pronounced "nice") is a common metamorphic rock, one recognized by its banded appearance. A good share of gneiss looks much like granite, which is what it was before pressures deep within the earth were applied. Ordinarily these pressures squeeze the rock from only one direction. In the Appalachians it was pressure from the eastern coast. As a result, rock crystals all become oriented in one direction, developing approximately at right angles to the pressures, rather than in line with them. The net effect is that the rock acquires a banded appearance, with the crystals forming parallel lines.

Some gneiss is formed when conglomerate is caught in mountain-building pressures, which causes the various stones composing the conglomerate to partially melt, becoming streaks of various types and colors, depending on the individual stones.

When shale is altered in mountain building, crystals are developed along the line of least resistance, away from the pressures, but the crystals in this case are tiny, not readily perceptible. The effect, though, becomes

Here are *hornblende* crystals in schist (on the left) and in pegmatite. Hornblende makes gabbro darker than granite. The crystals in rocks are seldom as well shaped as those shown here, but can be recognized by the tendency to develop such forms.

Here at the eastern edge of the Hudson Valley water from the mountainside freezes and tends to wedge rocks apart at the joints—one factor that causes mountains to be worn away.

apparent, for the rock formed is *slate,* which splits readily along the tiny crystals, not across them, and forms thin sheets that split easily in one direction. The thin sheets may break but will not split smoothly across the thin sheets.

Where the pressures on shale are more severe and long lasting, the crystals grow much larger, and the rock may become somewhat gnarled, forming *schist*. Much mica schist is readily visible in Central Park on Manhattan Island in New York City. It is known as "mica" schist because the mica crystals are quite large and prominent. Those crystals have all developed in the same direction, forming thin sheets of the mineral, one upon another. Such rocks are said to be "foliated," composed of tiny sheets, a characteristic common to many metamorphic rocks. Slate and mica schist are common in regions where mountain building has been severe and erosion has removed the rocks above.

Other types of schist include those named according to the predominant crystals, for example, hornblende schist and chlorite schist. Metamorphic rocks like mica schist in which the crystals are small but not as tiny as those in slate are called *phyllites.* Additionally, some schists are altered basalt.

Another metamorphic rock is *marble,* an altered form of limestone. The terms *limestone* and *marble* often are used loosely, and limestone is often called marble. In fact, marble is limestone that crystallized during an episode of mountain building. Crystals of calcite (lime) have been formed. Yet both limestone and marble are almost entirely lime.

One more kind of metamorphic rock should be noted: *quartzite,* an extremely hard rock converted from sandstone. Heat and pressure partially melt grains of sand until they fuse as a solid mass, with individual grains commonly remaining as glassy lumps within the quartzite mass. Mount Mitchell in the southern Appalachians is a prominent source.

The Weathering of Rock

When lava pours out onto the surface, it cools and shrinks, developing cracks, or joints. The type of jointing tends to be a characteristic of each kind of rock. Basalt, for example, has a tendency to develop six-sided columns. Granitoid rocks that cooled at great depths may later break as a result of the strains of continuing mountain-building pressures. Some masses of granite avoid jointing and persist as granite domes, such as those at Kings Canyon in California, but joints are common in most rocks. Sedimentary rocks shrink as they dry, and even the tremors of an earthquake may be enough to produce the strains that cause joints to develop.

Joints grow in many ways. On or near the surface, water will seep into the joints. In the winter, the water freezes, and the expansion due to freezing is sufficient to wedge rocks apart at the joints. The roots of trees and bushes often reach into joints for water and support. As the roots grow, they expand and help to force the rocks apart at the joints. In the mountains, when a mass of rock has been wedged apart sufficiently, part of it will tumble down the mountainside into a stream below. New boulders have sharp, broken edges. After a heavy rain, when the mountain streams become swift, the boulder will be rolled forward a bit with the current. Rolling over other stones, and with still more stones in the stream grinding against the broken edges, the boulder gradually becomes somewhat rounded. Smaller stones likewise come from bedrock, the sharp edges gradually becoming rounded in stream beds as the stones tumble over each other in the current.

Stones plucked off bedrock by a glacier can become frozen in the ice, in this way becoming somewhat flattened while being shoved along over solid rock at the base of the ice. If jolted loose, then frozen in another position, a second or even a third side may become flattened. Other stones may tumble down onto the surface of the ice and be carried to the terminus with little effect. Yet in glacial deposits, many are flattened and striated so that the source is readily identifiable. Glacial stones may be further transported in streams of meltwater from the ice. Glacial and stream-rounded stones in some cases may eventually become beach stones. These are shifted back and forth by the waves, becoming somewhat flattened by grinding back and forth over beach sands. Thus, beach stones tend to become flattened, thin and wafer shaped.

Rocks exposed to the weather tend to crumble, as seen here in West Virginia. In this case the hard rock surface is crumbling in what geologists call *exfoliation*.

As has been noted, limestone and marble gradually dissolve in the acids of the soil. To some extent other rocks also crumble on the surface when exposed to the elements, including the surface of open joints. Much as the sharp edges of an ice cube tend to become rounded, so do boulders and other broken stones, due to weathering. The result is termed *spheroidal weathering*. Or if the crumbling surface is flaking away, the process is known as *exfoliation*—something like removing the leaves of a cabbage or other plant. These rounded boulders are conspicuous in certain areas, such as on hillsides at Riverside, near Los Angeles, and in granite at the Joshua National Monument, also in southern California. Granite domes, such as Stone Mountain in Georgia, have become rounded masses as a result of the crumbling of exposed irregularities.

Less resistant rocks of all sizes merely crumble where exposed to weathering. Weakly cemented sandstone will crumble and once again become sand. Shale will crumble and again become clay. Slate and schist are more resistant, but eventually they too weather and become clay. In dry regions, windblown sand can erode the rocks, as in Bryce Canyon, but wind is not much of a factor except in deserts.

How to Recognize Rocks

Rocks can be identified in a variety of ways. Look to see if there are lines of stratification to indicate a sedimentary rock. Igneous rocks are massive, and metamorphic rocks are foliated with lines made by crystals. The lines of stratification on a sedimentary rock are made by sediments that settled out of water, and those tend to be gradual changes as one flood subsided before another gradually began. The lines in metamorphic rocks are made by crystals in the rock; hence they are more distinct than those in a stratified rock. Also, metamorphic rocks frequently show crumpling or folding resulting from the pressures that altered the rock. Felsitic rocks tend to be somewhat larger and are much harder. Limestone seldom shows clear lines of stratification, even though it is sedimentary. Lime settles out of deep water farther from shore than sand or clay; hence seasonal variations in the type of sediment are less distinct.

Weathering ordinarily obscures the surface of any rock exposed by the roadside or found as a loose stone. So weathered stones must be broken or chipped to obtain a fresh surface for examination. Incidentally, identification of a loose stone has little value, whereas the same effort applied to solid rock can reveal the story of the land in that area. For example, if the bedrock is found to be metamorphic, it would indicate mountain building there. Or if limestone is found, it would indicate that the region had been under water at some time in the past. A loose stone reveals nothing beyond itself.

Limestone may look something like clay or shale, although the clay or shale may have fine lines of stratification where mud settled out of water. If in doubt, use the blade of a pocketknife to scrape away the weathered surface, then scrape a little more to get a bit of powdered rock. With a moistened finger, place a bit of the powder on your tongue. Clay or shale will taste like mud, limestone like chalk.

In some cases it may be difficult to distinguish massive sandstone from an igneous rock. If necessary, use a magnifying glass to examine the crystals. In an igneous rock the crystals will be sharp and angular, but those of a sedimentary rock will be somewhat rounded, as if having been in a stream.

Most gneiss can be readily distinguished from schist. The schist is likely to be more uniform in appearance, except when it includes white quartz. In schist the foliation, the sheetlike appearance of crystals, will be more evident than in gneiss, which is more obviously banded.

Clay and shale are so much alike that in many cases it may be hard to tell one from another. One thing to remember is that shale is a cemented rock, whereas clay is not. So place a specimen in water for a while. If it dissolves to form mud, it was clay. If not, it is shale.

Likewise, shale can be difficult to distinguish from slate. To tell one from the other, look for lines of stratification maintained from the original sediment. If the rock has split smoothly along those lines, it is shale. In slate, the cleavage usually is at a sharp angle to those original lines. But such lines may not be readily apparent. If the rock is being examined where it was formed, look for evidence of folding. If the cleavage, the splitting, is in line with the folds, the rock is shale, but if it splits across the folds, it is slate. In one case the rock is splitting along the lines of stratification; in the other it splits along the fine crystals formed in metamorphosis. In shale the lines of stratification are also likely to blend gradually from one to the other, but the cleavage of slate is more sharply defined. Slate usually is somewhat harder than shale, but the hardness may be difficult to determine accurately.

Felsite and quartzite are also quite similar. Quartzite is a fused quartz, and quartz is hard, but felsites are largely quartz too. The lumpy grains of the glassy quartzite may be evident, or the flow lines of the volcanic felsite. Quartzite may be a bit harder, as it is more nearly pure quartz; if one sample is rubbed against the other with force, the quartzite will scratch the felsite. If both are not available, a difference may be detected with a pocketknife.

Conglomerate can be distinguished from the lava, breccia, by examining the rocks' content. In lava flows, a top crust may cool and harden. With a further surge of lava, the crust may be broken and engulfed, forming a rock containing broken fragments of the same lava. Conglomerate is a rock containing rounded pebbles.

If limestone must be distinguished from marble, look for crystals in the marble, or mere granules in limestone. Some evidence of folding also will distinguish the marble. If fossils within the rock have been streaked or contorted, the rock is obviously metamorphic, a marble.

Distinguishing one mineral from another can be complex. Yet some distinctions can be quite evident and helpful in the identification of rocks. In granite, for example, the quartz is glassy and hard. Because quartz is common and readily identified, it should become familiar. Minerals are identified by the shapes of their crystals, but in most cases the minerals in a rock are crowded and not in ideal shape. Quartz, for example, forms glassy, six-sided crystals that come to a point at the free end. But in sandstone the grains of quartz have become worn and rounded. Although ordinarily glasslike in appearance, veins of quartz are far more likely to be milky white with no evidence of crystalline form. Even so, distinctions are readily made by the hardness and the familiar appearance in a vein.

Gold, for example, is often falsely identified, confused with pyrite, which is known as "fool's gold." Pyrite may be found in cubes or other well-formed crystals. Those crystals are quite hard, although not as hard as quartz. Pyrite crystals have a metallic sheen, and the color is much like that of gold. But whereas pyrite is hard and in distinct crystals, gold is very soft and amorphous (except where mixed with other metals in jewelry), having no distinct form. Crystalline form, or the lack of it, and hardness are the distinctive qualities of gold and pyrite.

In their laboratories, mineralogists can determine the precise density of any pure mineral. Gold is far heavier than pyrite. The specific gravity (density) of gold is 19.3, pyrite 5.1, with gold almost four times as heavy as an equal volume of pyrite. In the field that distinction may not be made with precision, though the knowledge that gold is especially heavy for its size, and that density is a distinctive feature of all minerals, can be meaningful. In movie westerns, when a stagecoach is robbed and the bandit blithely steals away with a large chest of gold, something more than thievery is wrong. A chest full of gold, almost 20 times as heavy as a like amount of water, would be difficult—if not impossible—to lift!

The feldspar in granite has a milky-white or somewhat red cast with a surface sheen similar to that of a dinner plate—not a surprising similarity in that the glaze on a plate is made from feldspar. Crystalline forms are difficult to determine in a rock, except for the flat surface of a feldspar crystal. Good specimens of feldspar crystals are obtained from pegmatite, a granitelike rock with large crystals.

In addition to weight and appearance, mineralogists have a hardness scale, called the Mohs scale after the man who devised it, to serve as an identification guide. Talc (from which talcum powder is made) is number one, soft enough to be scraped with a fingernail. Gypsum, a bit harder, is number two on the scale, and calcite (lime) is number three. Calcite crystals are colorless and glasslike but much softer than quartz, which is number seven on the scale—the hardest of very common minerals. Fluorite and apatite are four and five on the scale. Feldspar is number six, not quite as hard as quartz yet as hard or harder than most other minerals. Topaz and corundum are harder at eight and nine on the scale. Hardest of all is number ten, diamond. Diamonds are so hard, imperfect crystals serve as industrial abrasives. With calcite, feldspar, and quartz, numbers three, six, and seven on the scale, it is possible to determine the approximate hardness of any specimen, using these to see which will scratch the specimen and how readily it does so. A knife blade can also be used instead. The hardness of a knife varies with the quality of the steel but is likely to be somewhere between the five of apatite and the six of feldspar. The hardness of glass is about the same. If the knife blade will not scratch the mineral, that mineral must have the hardness of feldspar or even quartz. If the specimen can be scratched with a knife, that mineral may be a four or five on the scale, depending upon how easily scratched. Calcite, number three on the scale, will scratch easily but not with a fingernail.

The color of a mineral can give a clue, but color can be a misleading guide. For example, there are many varieties of quartz with different colors. The colors come from other minerals, impurities, diffused throughout the glasslike quartz. Pure quartz is a definite compound, SiO_2, just as calcite is CaCO₃. Yet quartz can have a smoky appearance when carbon is diffused throughout the crystal, or a rusty brown with iron oxide. Some impure quartz is valuable in its own right: Amethyst is quartz with manganese to give it a violet color. Where quartz has formed in the crowded confines of a rock, perfect crystals cannot form, and the result may be a mass that is milky white. Mineralogists have still another way of identifying quartz. It is known as "fracture," in this case "concoidal fracture." If a mass of quartz, or felsite that contains much quartz, is chipped, it will have a shell-like surface beginning at the point of fracture—somewhat distorted concentric circles, like waves spreading from the point where broken.

In granite the dark minerals are mica, hornblende, or augite. Mica is a semitransparent mineral in thin sheets. The mica crystals in mica schist are likely to be larger than those in granite. Hornblenden forms six-sided crystals but may be in grains or masses that are black, dark brown, or a greenish black. Augite is similar in color but with odd-shaped crystals somewhat askew. Both augite and hornblende tend to have a surface sheen like that of a well-polished pair of black shoes.

Determining the Years Involved in Changes

As we have seen, geologists can tell the sequence of events in sedimentary rocks by superposition. Sediments on top are more recent than the ones below. If lava pours out onto the sediments, the lava is still more recent. Or if molten rock is forced up through the sediments, the sediments are older. These methods are still good, but they give little if any idea regarding how long changes may have taken. Yet erosion and the deposition of sediments on floodplains go on all the time; so geologists have made rough estimates of how long it would take to wear down a mountain or fill a valley with sediment. Such estimates were quite inadequate but are better now than people previously had assumed. During the Middle Ages in Europe it was believed the world was only about 6,000 years old. Modern scientists put the age of the Earth at 4 ½ billion to 5 billion years.

What are these newer methods? Radioactivity is the key. When it was discovered that uranium and certain other minerals give off radiation, scientists began experimenting to see what that radiation was. They learned that each radioactive mineral emits radiation at a uniform rate, but some minerals emit radiation more rapidly than others. In each case the radiation from a given mineral grows weaker at a uniform rate. It was found that each mineral will lose half its radiation in a certain number of years—or days, or minutes, or seconds. Uranium will emit half its radiation in 4 ½ billion years. After that time the radiation given off by the uranium will be only half what it was at the beginning. After another 4 ½ billion years the rate again will be diminished by half, which means it will be only a fourth as much as at the beginning. Theoretically there is no end to it. The radiation gradually weakens at the uniform rate. These vast periods of time for the half-life of uranium indicate very little change in a human lifetime, but the slow rate has been ideal for estimating the great age of the Earth. With it we find that uranium formed when the Earth was created has lost half the intensity of radiation it originally had.

There are elements that are much more radioactive than uranium. Some are so highly radioactive that they emit half their radiation in minutes, even seconds. Such elements are never around long enough to bother anyone, or to be useful either, but elements with radiation rates somewhere between these extremes have been found to be very useful in a great number of ways. Hospitals soon discovered that for medical use, radium, with a half-life of 1,590 years, is ideal. Radium emits a highly radioactive gas, radon, which can be used for medical diagnosis and therapy, preserving the precious radium itself for future use.

A small fraction of potassium, K40, emits radiation and disintegrates to a residual, inactive argon at a half-life rate of 1,310 years, which provides a convenient measurement for many geological formations and archaeological sites. Carbon-14 represents but a small portion of the total carbon extant, yet that portion has been radioactive with a half-life of 5,570 years. If this rate is known, the age of carbon in the ashes of a Stone Age fire can be determined. No carbon has been added since the original fire, so the radiation remaining in the ashes gives an accurate estimate of the years since the wood was burned.

Such estimates based on known rates of radiation are now used widely to reveal the number of years in geological time. For example, the Cambrian Period, with the first conspicuous evidence of life on Earth, began about 600 million years ago; the Appalachians were uplifted about 230 million years ago; the Rockies, 70 million years ago.

How Fossils Are Formed

Fossils are most common in sedimentary rocks; the relatively stable conditions under which these rocks form are quite conducive to fossiliza-

Rounded colonies of seaweed such as this are found as fossils at the southeastern edge of the Adirondacks in New York. This seaweed fossil, a form of algae, is among the oldest, most primitive forms of life known.

tion. Seashells, for example, are often found in limestone. The limestone itself may come from the disintegration of shells and from the lime in the skeletons of innumerable tiny organisms. Coral reefs are made in this way, from the accumulation of layers of skeletal remains sinking as lime. When waves destroy some reefs, the fragments settle further to the bottom, becoming consolidated over time as limestone, along with the shells and body parts of other creatures that eventually die in the water. Even fish, lobsters, and other such animals sink to the bottom when they die and become enmeshed in the accumulating sediment. In the case of the largely boneless sharks, only the teeth are preserved. The flesh may be eaten by other animals or may decay. Bones and shells are more readily preserved in the lime and thus become fossils in limestone. A great variety of fossils can be found in limestone.

Shale is another good source of fossils, for reasons similar to limestone. When mud washes into the sea, it settles to the bottom some distance from shore but not as far out as the lime that becomes limestone. The clay that becomes shale thus contains fossils much like those of limestone, though since it rests closer to shore, shale is likely to have more plant fossils and fewer shells. Even fish, if not eaten when they die, may fall to the bottom to be preserved as fossils. Since shale, like limestone, is composed of fine particles, shale fossils often show fine details of plant and animal forms. In the shales of the Hudson River valley, for example, some fine specimens of graptolites, an extinct wormlike hydrozoan that had no bones, no shell, or any other hard parts, are preserved. The only vestige of the animal's body is imprinted black carbon, the result of partial decay under water. All that is known about these extinct slender creatures, about two inches or less in length, comes from their fossil imprints in the shale.

Most sandstone is quite coarse in comparison with shale or limestone and so is not likely to show as fine detail. Yet since it is formed closer to shore, sandstone may contain more plant fossils, such as palm leaves or the fronds of ferns that may have been growing along a bank. Some sandstones are quite coarse, but the finer siltstones can show good detail. At the other extreme, conglomerate seldom contains discernible fossils. Dinosaur footprints have been discovered in Connecticut and Texas sandstone, and their bones have been found in Rocky Mountain sandstone as well as the shale of the former lowland. In the Petrified Forest, decaying wood that gained minerals from the water has been preserved in sandstone.

Ordinarily, nobody expects to find fossils in igneous or metamorphic rocks, due to the turbulent processes that produce them. Yet there are exceptions. When limestone is converted to marble, some fossils may remain discernible, although heat and pressure will have caused some distortions. In granite or other igneous rocks there will be no fossils. In lava, however, something may occasionally be engulfed in the flow. During lava flows, plant leaves may become fossil imprints in the hardened rock. Sometimes, too, plants growing in clay may become fossil imprints in the clay once it is converted to rock, a hornfel, due to the heat of the overriding lava, an example of contact metamorphism.

Abandoned strip mines in coal-mining areas are excellent places to find fossils. They are likely to be quite safe, and since the good coal has been removed, what remains quite often contains shale with fossils. Coal is formed in swamplike conditions where plants fall into shallow water and partially decay. Where conditions are not quite right for the production of coal, it may be just right for the preservation of fossils. With the marketable coal removed, what remains may have developed during the transition conditions before or after the coal was forming, and these may yield fossils of the same age as those of the coal forests. Underground mines often do reveal fossils, but these and operating surface mines are not as safe or accessible. On the border of Virginia and West Virginia, west of Bluefield, West Virginia, the Pocahontas Exhibition Mine, no longer operational, is open to the public, and visitors can see large, conspicuous fossils in the walls and ceiling of the mine.

Another good place to find fossils is a limestone quarry, provided it is safe and not flooded with deep water. Broken fragments of limestone may be found in a trash heap, discarded as not suitable for construction purposes, and those fragments may contain fossils.

In banks by the roadside, where the roads have been cut through shale, limestone, or sandstone, fossils frequently can be found. Unfortunately, stopping to examine the banks of rock beside a superhighway is commonly prohibited, though there are a number of other roads that parallel the expressways. In addition to the plant and animal fossils that may be found along roadways, there may be fossil mud cracks, where mud in what once was a lowland shrank and cracked as it dried, though leaving sufficient moisture for the chemical processes that convert clay to shale or lime to limestone to occur.

Ripple marks found in shale or fine sandstone indicate that shallow water covered the land and that brisk winds blowing across the water produced ripples in the water reaching down into the sand or mud below. Similar conditions along a shore can be seen today, but in most cases the ripples are obliterated without becoming fossilized. If fossilized ripple marks are found, note the direction the wind was blowing at the time the ripples were formed.

By no means rare, yet not as common or conspicuous, are fossil raindrops in shale or siltstone. They may look like pockmarks at first, but the rounded depressions indicate a sudden, brief shower with large drops. Prolonged rain would have obliterated the impressions. In this case, too, notice the direction of the wind, as indicated by deeper impressions on the leeward side. If the imprint is slightly deeper and steeper on the

These fossilized raindrops in fine sandstone were made during a brief but heavy shower long ago in the Connecticut Valley. The indentations are steeper on one side, indicating the rain was falling at an angle, most likely due to a strong southwest wind.

northeast side, a southwest wind is indicated, with the raindrops slanting down from the southwest.

The Significance of Fossils

Fossils can tell us how life developed on Earth and can sharpen our views of when events occurred. For example, we now know that frozen Antarctica once had a temperate climate with forests. Fossils have helped in developing the concept of plate tectonics and drifting continents. Similarities in fossils along with other comparisons have helped to show that South America and Africa once were joined. Likewise, fossils provide evidence that West Coast terranes are distinct from their surroundings and at the same time indicate where those parcels of land originated and how far they have drifted to merge with North America. Oil drillers watch the fossils they encounter closely to see if their efforts will result in prosperity or only an expensive dry hole.

For geologists, one of the more valuable uses of fossils is the correlation of strata. If the fossils typical of those in the Grand Canyon at a certain depth are like those in an isolated layer of rock elsewhere, the two obviously are of the same age, the same sequence in development. Fossils typical of a given age, ideal for such correlations, are termed *index fossils*. Without them, findings throughout the world would remain unrelated, and geology would be left with a jumble of largely isolated facts. When a new skeleton is discovered, its location in the surrounding strata is highly significant. The fossils where the discovery was made provide a means of dating the human remains, even before anthropologists begin to analyze the physical features and apparent stage of development.

Some Fossil Sites

Conveniently located on the east side of Route 5 in the Connecticut Valley of Massachusetts are fossil footprints of dinosaurs, preserved by the state. These tracks are large and show long strides from one step to the next, yet the Triassic dinosaurs there were not as large as the ones that developed in the next geological period, the Jurassic. The tracks are in fine sandstone, originally made in sand about 230 million years ago.

Another such display of dinosaur tracks, on property belonging to Yale University, is a short distance southeast of Meriden, Connecticut. These tracks are somewhat more difficult to locate, off Route 147, near Baileyville on a side road leading to the southeast.

Still another location in Connecticut, Dinosaur State Park, is on Route 91 between Meriden and Hartford. This park features a large number of tracks made by dinosaurs estimated to have been eight feet tall and 20 feet long.

In New York City, the American Museum of Natural History has fabulous displays of dinosaurs. Some are so large that no ordinary building could hold them. The actual bones stand erect as if truly alive. Brontosaurus, Tyrannosaurus, and the others stand there, the magnificent displays occupying many spacious rooms and including fossils of other kinds as well.

Also worth a visit is the Dinosaur National Monument on the Colorado Plateau, where huge behemoths died in a sandy streambed before the plateau was uplifted. From Salt Lake City, Route 40 leads east to Vernal,

Utah, and on to Jensen where a side road goes to the visitors center for the monument. The national monument extends far beyond the state line into Colorado. Here are huge dinosaur bones in the ground where they were found, uncovered but otherwise undisturbed. At the visitors center a large building has been constructed to shelter many of the bones, but far more are outside near the building and beyond throughout the extensive monument. In becoming fossilized, living tissue has been replaced by minerals from the water that once covered the bones in lowland sand, but the minerals of the bones remain unchanged.

The Ice Age fossils of the La Brea Tar Pits in Los Angeles, mentioned in chapter 3, likewise provide a good view of animal life in the more recent past. Another such fossil site is Big Bone Lick State Park in Kentucky, southwest of Florence. Enticed by a salt lick there, a great variety of Ice Age animals became entrapped in a deep bog, including more than 100 mastodons.

In the state of Washington, seashells can be found in the rocks above the water level of flat-topped islands throughout Puget Sound and also along the Pacific coast. This and other evidence indicates that the land has risen and is apparently still doing so. At the same time, the fact that Puget Sound is a drowned system of river valleys indicates the basin there has been depressed, folded downward between the mountain ranges on each side, even though more recently springing part way back up.

On a rocky cliff overlooking the waters of Puget Sound some fossil palms rest in solid rock. The location is close to Bellingham, Washington, on Chuckanut Drive, about 50 miles from the Canadian border. The climate there is mild but far from the tropical conditions essential for palms. Evidently the climate has changed drastically, or else the mountain there has drifted northward from the tropics. The fossil palms are easy to see, in rock beside a highway leading north into Bellingham.

As noted in the first chapter, the ginkgo State Park in Washington is east of the Cascade Range beyond Ellensburg off Route 90, overlooking the Columbia River. There the stumps of ginkgo trees have been preserved in their original positions where they had been originally growing, now petrified by minerals from the lava that engulfed them. Only the stumps were covered and thus petrified. Ginkgo trees are quite distinctive. They were common during the Jurassic Period when dinosaurs were predominant in the Mesozoic Era, but were thought to be extinct like the dinosaurs. Fifteen million years or more ago, these trees were part of a verdant forest in a temperate climate. Then the forest was inundated with repeated, extensive lava flows followed by the uplift of the Cascade Range. Elevation of the mountains completely changed the climate to that of a semidesert characteristic of the region today. The fossils help testify to this change of climate and living conditions in the region and provide further evidence of the influence mountains have on life even today.

East of the Grand Canyon in Arizona, off Route 40, where the Petrified Forest National Park is located, there once was a large lowland stream before the Rocky Mountains and Colorado Plateau were uplifted. The logs that have become petrified there apparently were uprooted trees washed downstream during major floods and left in a jumbled mass at a bend in the river, an eddy, along with a great mass of colorful sand—sand like that of the adjoining Painted Desert. Like most sand, that of the desert is bits of quartz eroded from granite and other such rocks. The distinctive feature in this case is that the sand contains traces of various colorful minerals. In becoming petrified those minerals have seeped into the logs, replacing the decaying wood bit by bit, so that the logs have become colorful, like the sands of the Painted Desert.

The fossil tree stumps discovered at Gilboa in the Catskills are those of trees from the oldest forest known. Some of the fossils can be seen in displays by the roadside there in the Catskills. An account of how these early fossils were found and what the land was like when the trees were alive accompanies featured displays at the New York State Museum in Albany.

Tree ferns like those now fossilized at Gilboa grow only in the tropics today. Whereas only the stumps were preserved as fossils at Gilboa, farther west at Naples, New York, a more nearly complete fossil tree was found and is now on display at the state museum, along with a restoration showing how it looked when alive. The Naples tree was not a tree fern like those at Gilboa, but a giant club moss. No such trees exist today. The nearest surviving relative is "ground pine," which is not a pine tree but a vine trailing along the ground in patches, in the open woods.

At the time of such Paleozoic trees, there were no modern trees such as pine and other conifers, or deciduous trees such as maples and oaks. But tree ferns and club moss trees were common in the coal forests that produced the coal we mine today. Numerous fossils of these ancient trees are exposed in coal mines. If looking for such fossils in strip mines,

On this limb of a fossil tree are leaf scars, indicating where other leaves were attached. A cast of the limb was preserved in the sandstone of a strip mine near Elkins, West Virginia. Strange trees grew in the coal forests, such as this giant club moss, known as a scale tree.

a good place to begin is along Highway 79 south of Pittsburgh, but such mines are common throughout West Virginia, eastern Kentucky, and eastern Ohio, or wherever coal is mined. The Pocahontas Exhibition Mine is at Pocahontas, Virginia, on Route 102, near the state line west of Bluefield, West Virginia. Fossil tree trunks are readily visible in the mine near the entrance.

It is obviously impossible to list all the places where fossils can be found. At Glacier Park in Montana the emphasis is on glaciation, but there is more to be seen. The rocks of the mountains have developed from sediments in an ancient depression that extends north and south throughout the current Rocky Mountain region. Now that the former lowland has been elevated to form massive mountains, fossil mud cracks in shale and the ripple marks of shallow water formed in a lowland remain to tell what conditions were like. But of the fossils, the most noted are the fossilized colonies of algae. These are among the oldest living things known. Similar fossils are exhibited at the Adirondacks in New York, but those in Montana may be even more ancient, in fact Precambrian. The extensive masses of fossilized calcareous algae can be found in rounded masses on the surface near the Grinnell Glacier, but the beds are reported to be 60 feet deep. The extensive beds create a distinctive light gray band on the mountains.

Approaching the northwest corner of Yellowstone Park from Bozeman, Route 191 passes a petrified forest, conveniently located for seeing more fossils. Yellowstone Park is mostly a high plateau built of lava in great depths, exhibiting abundant evidence of continuing volcanic activity. Forests there were buried to great depths by volcanic ash from intermittent eruptions. Minerals permeated the trunks as the wood decayed, thus forming petrified wood, fossil trees with their tops gone, the trunks preserved by minerals from the volcanic ash.

In the lava fields of Idaho's Craters of the Moon National Monument there are numerous tree molds. Where the lava flowed into a forest, the lava was cooled and hardened in contact with the wet sap at the base of the tree, preserving the form of the trunk as a mold. The wood burned, and whatever remained decayed. The molds remain as holes in the lava beds where the tree stood.

Many kinds of fossils are common and not difficult to find, yet occasionally something spectacular is encountered. In an abandoned quarry at North Bergen, across the Hudson River from New York City, in 1960 three New Jersey high school boys discovered a unique fossil. The boys had been looking through the rocks of the quarry when they came across the almost complete remains of a certain extinct reptile—a flying lizard. No such animal had ever been seen before, and their find is now on display at the American Museum of Natural History in New York City, named after one of the boys who made the discovery.

8

MOUNTAINS OF THE PAST

The oldest mountain range in North America, of which adequate evidence remains, is the Laurentian Range of southern Canada. From north of Lake Superior the old range extends eastward on the north side of the Saint Lawrence Valley to the east coast of Labrador. In Labrador, the mountains remain prominent to this day, although badly worn. Farther west all that remains are the ancient hard rocks of the Laurentian upland, worn almost flat. North of the Great Lakes, the stumps of these mountains are all that provide evidence of the once-great mountain range. In northern Wisconsin and central Minnesota there are rock formations that indicate that the old mountain range extended farther west. In South Dakota the Black Hills are a more recent uplift of very old rocks that also could have been a continuation of the Laurentian Range. Rocks of the same age are found in the Grand Canyon, suggesting that the former mountains extended across the entire continent to what was the west coast of that early time.

In the two billion years since the Laurentians were uplifted there have been many changes. Erosion cut down the original mountains, but the mountain range was reelevated during the Algoman Revolution. As time went by, those mountains likewise were worn away; they were eventually uplifted again in the Killarney Revolution. In this way, the hard rocks from deep within mountains are left at the surface, in this case across southern Canada with traces westward into the United States.

The erosion of a great mountain range continuing over a very long expanse of time produces vast amounts of sediment. No doubt much of that sediment is washed away, leaving no trace, but tremendous amounts have accumulated in some locations. A prime example is the so-called Grenville System of metamorphic sediments in southeastern Ontario, southern Quebec, along the St. Lawrence Valley, and in the Adirondack Mountains of New York. The altered sediments are said to be thousands of feet deep, consisting largely of schists, sandstones, and crystalline limestones formed from the original clay, sand, and lime from the old mountains.

The same pressures that rebuilt the mountains converted the sediments to metamorphic rocks. As the mountains were being reelevated, the layered sediments were intruded by lavas and upwelling granite in a complex series of uplifts, erosion, and metamorphism. The time intervals were immense, so that trees and other vegetation developed on the eroded surfaces and deposits of sediment, as indicated by abundant carbon found in the layered rocks. No doubt the vegetation was destroyed as mountain building resumed, and the carbon from the plants was converted to graphite, which is pure carbon familiar to most of us as the "lead" in pencils.

The Adirondack Mountains, separated from Canada by the St. Lawrence lowland and from Vermont by the fault line occupied by Lake Champlain, are geologically considered an extension of the Laurentian Highlands of Canada, quite distinct from the Appalachians of New England. Like the Laurentians, the Adirondacks consist of rock formations older than those of the Appalachians. The Adirondacks have been worn down, but the worn surface was reelevated along with the Appalachians. Subsequently erosion has shaped the Adirondacks and continues to do so.

Where the Adirondacks border the Champlain lowland, evidence remains of pressures from the east that elevated the mountains to their present heights. From the Mohawk Valley, Routes 87 and 9N go north to Saratoga Springs; just beyond Glens Falls at the city of Lake George, Route 9N runs beside the 32-mile-long, narrow Lake George. The lake occupies a fault zone where rocks were broken as the mountains were reelevated. It is noteworthy that many other lakes in the vicinity also are long and narrow, oriented in the same north-south direction and located in faults, indicating that the mountain-building pressures were from the east.

Like the Laurentians, the Adirondacks have gone through interminable changes, uplifts, and erosions throughout their long history. Today the mountains consist of granitoid rocks along with a jumble of former sediments altered during subsequent uplifts. What had been sand or sandstone is now very hard quartzite. The crystalline schist of today was originally mud, then clay, hardened to shale. What had been lime became limestone, but unlike the resistant surrounding rocks, limestone crumbles in acid, leaving an irregular surface wherever exposed. During the repeated uplifts, even the granite intrusions under one-sided pressure were changed to a banded metamorphic rock, gneiss. Having been worn almost flat before the most recent uplift, evidence of that old worn surface is apparent in the summit of the Adirondacks. The more westerly summits are of uniform height and have an appearance much like that of an eroded plateau.

The Black Hills of South Dakota are somewhat like the Adirondacks. An apparent extension of the Laurentian Range, the uplift is a mass of old rocks with the rounded shape of a dome, although considerably longer east to west than rocks of the original mountain range. The central core of the region is composed of granite and other crystalline rocks surrounded by a rim of limestone. Outside the main uplift is a rounded lowland with an upturned outer edge of hard sandstone. Apparently the surrounding sandstone of the Great Plains was tilted upward with the revived uplift of the old rocks at the core. Outside the main dome of old rock are some more recent intrusions of igneous rock, forming surrounding hills. These apparently were formed by upwelling magma during the revived uplift of the ancient rocks.

Duluth, Minnesota, is located on a highland overlooking the southern tip of Lake Superior. There, northwest of Lake Superior, is a broad expanse of ridges extending northeastward into Canada. The rocks of the highland are the exposed remains of the Laurentian Mountains. In this location the rocks contain rich deposits of iron and other metal ores. The ores are found as sedimentary deposits formed while the old mountains were being eroded. This outstanding source of iron ore is now located at the surface of what is known as the Mesabi Range. The parallel Vermillion Range is another bountiful source. Still other rich sources of iron ore from old mountains are south of Lake Superior, where underground mining is necessary to reach the deposits, and farther north along the Quebec-Labrador border. Somewhat less noted yet extremely valuable copper ore is located on the north side of Lake Superior. Also near Sudbury, Ontario, there are valuable ores of nickel and copper, as well as veins of silver, gold, and cobalt.

The Canadian Shield, which includes most of Canada, except for the mountains of the west, is a flat surface of bare rock. Interlocking igneous and metamorphic rocks are the kinds formed deep within now-eroded mountains. Despite the harsh northern climate, such rocks are resistant to weathering, though they are quite bare, scoured by the accumulation of snow compacted to ice, which then scraped the surface as massive glaciers.

The complex expanse of crystalline rocks plainly represents the roots of ancient mountains but reveals no systematic clues to these mountains, the evidence lost in a succession of ancient upheavals. Of one thing geologists are sure. The rocks are very old, many of them dating from nearly the beginnings of the Earth and the solar system. Ordinarily, fossils found in rocks help to identify the geological period in which they were formed. But there are no fossils in these rocks, which indicates that the rocks were formed deep within mountains and apparently also long before life developed, even very primitive forms such as algae.

Through the use of radioactive elements such as uranium 238, which decay at precise, known rates, geologists are able to date even the oldest rocks. Uranium has a half-life of 4.5 billion years, which means that half of a given sample will decay over that time. Uranium is common in igneous rock; wherever U 238 is found, knowing how much has disintegrated will reveal the age of the rocks. Other radioactive minerals in the rocks can be used in like manner to date rocks.

Some of the oldest rocks anywhere are in southwestern Greenland, known to be a little more than 3.8 billion years old. The rocks of the Laurentian Mountains in Labrador are about the same age, which is not surprising in that Canada and Greenland were united in the distant past and are still close today. Following the plate tectonics model, it is believed that Greenland and Labrador separated at about the same time that Africa was withdrawing from the Appalachian region of North America. In Minnesota, rocks from the base of the ancient Laurentian Mountains have been dated at about 3 ⅓ billion years old. With the Earth itself known to be about 4 ½ billion years old, the original Laurentian Mountains and certain other rocks of the Canadian Shield were formed not long after the Earth itself solidified.

To get a glimpse of these old rocks, travelers can cross the continent by way of the Trans-Canada Highway. From Vancouver, British Columbia, the highway cuts through scenic mountains to Calgary, Alberta, then across the Great Plains to Regina, Saskatchewan, and Winnipeg, Manitoba. North of Lake Huron, the highway divides, Route 17 to North Bay continuing north to the Canadian interior, then eastward to Ottawa, then Montreal. Proceeding northeast along the south side of the St. Lawrence River to Quebec City provides a fine view of the Laurentian Upland on which the city is built. These heights are all that remains of the old Laurentian Mountains.

Many spectacular views of the Canadian west can be seen from the Alaskan Highway. The highway begins at Dawson Creek, British Columbia, and proceeds northward through the Yukon Territory into Alaska. Highway 97 out of Washington leads northward to Prince George, then to Dawson Creek, where the designated highway begins. In southern British Columbia, west of Calgary and north of Vancouver, Highway 1, the Trans-Canada Highway, merges with Route 97, providing a convenient route north from the east or from Vancouver and other points in the far west.

Another option, featuring striking views of west coast mountains and glaciers, is passage on a cruise ship along the coast of Canada and among the islands of southern Alaska, a route known as the "Inside Passage."

9

MIDOCEAN RIDGES AND TERRANES

Early in 1975, newspapers and magazines featured accounts of a volcanic eruption in Iceland, an island in the North Atlantic between Greenland and Scandinavia. The eruption occurred on a small island off the southern coast, a new volcano on the outskirts of a fishing village of 5,000 people, at a spot where a Christian shrine was located. Accordingly, the volcano was named Kirkjufell, which means "church mountain."

One night before dawn, without warning, flames burst from the ground along a line that bulged and split open as if cut by a dull knife. Soon a wall of flame was rising high into the air with glowing chunks of rock, black cinders, and white steam forming an immense cloud above the island. The darkened sky was lighted by flashes of lightning from the cloud. Thunder followed, and at the same time rumbling sounds came from deep inside the volcano.

In a few days a volcanic mountain peak had formed out of the ash that settled down, together with chunks of rock and masses of lava. As the new volcano continued to erupt, the peak grew taller. Deep layers of black ash settled over houses and streets; glowing lava engulfed many buildings at the edge of town. Town inhabitants were evacuated by air and by sea. Some of the houses were completely buried under ash; others were burned by glowing masses of rock hurled from the mouth of the volcano.

Still other buildings were crushed by an advancing wall of lava. The hot rock then caused the rubble to burn.

With dark clouds overhead obscuring the light, and ash settling down like rain, the rumbling of the new mountain created an eerie atmosphere that seemed otherworldly. Lava flowed down the slope through the edge of town and into the harbor. Within three months, more than half a square mile of black rock was added to the island.

The Mid-Atlantic Ridge

Ten years earlier, off the southern shore of Iceland, the crew of a fishing boat observed the emergence of a new volcanic island. The eruption began under water with steam, black ash, and sulfur fumes rising to the surface, disturbing the water surface and forming a great cloud above the water. Within a day the tip of a volcano emerged from the water forming a new island named Surtsey. The volcano continued to erupt intermittently for several years, with lava flows. Today Surtsey is a stable island about a mile wide, rising several hundred feet above the water.

Much farther south, in the middle of the Atlantic Ocean, is Tristan da Cunha, the peak of an old volcano, now a small island. The island is in the South Atlantic, half way between South America and the southern tip of Africa. In 1961, when the volcanic island began to erupt again, the 262 islanders had to abandon their homes.

Saint Helena, the island where Napoleon died in exile, is also entirely volcanic. Like Tristan da Cunha, this larger island is in the mid-Atlantic, 1,200 miles off the coast of Africa.

Also in the mid-Atlantic, north of Saint Helena and Tristan da Cunha, are the Ascension Islands, also volcanic. Northward toward Iceland are the Azores, a line of nine volcanic islands. In fact, the mid-Atlantic is dotted with volcanic islands. Although larger than the other mid-Atlantic islands, as large as the state of Kentucky, Iceland too is made entirely of lava. Numerous volcanoes continue to be active there. A great rift valley along which volcanoes erupt cuts across the middle of the island. Like a city street bounded by tall buildings, the rift valley is bordered by walls of rock formed as pressures from below have broken through, lifting the sides higher than the middle. As lava continues to rise with each eruption, new rock is added at the middle, and in this way the island is expanding.

These volcanic islands all share a common origin—the Mid-Atlantic Ridge. Oceanographers have found that Iceland and other volcanic islands are merely the tops of mountain peaks standing above a long, rugged mountain range at the middle of the Atlantic Ocean. Like Iceland, the underwater range has a rift valley at the middle with walls of jagged rock on each side. There hot, molten rock rises from the depths to widen the rift. As the rift widens, the solid rocks of the ocean floor on each side are moved farther apart. As Iceland and the entire North Atlantic are widened, Greenland is moved a little farther from northern Europe. Likewise in the Atlantic farther south, as the Mid-Atlantic Ridge widens,

MIDOCEAN RIDGES AND TERRANES

North America drifts farther from the coast of Africa. In the South Atlantic, Africa and South America are gradually moving apart in a similar way. The Atlantic is expanding only about an inch or so each year, but over a 200-million-year period the Atlantic has become a great ocean, and the gradual movement continues.

Interestingly, the Appalachian Mountains, which now extend from Alabama along the east coast into Nova Scotia and Newfoundland, once continued on through the British Isles and the Scandinavian Peninsula. But these portions of the old mountain range are now separated by the ever widening North Atlantic Ocean.

Today Africa is pressing against southern Europe, narrowing the Mediterranean Sea and thrusting the rocks of Europe upward to form the Alps. Looking back 200 million years, we find North America bordered on the east by Africa and on the north by western Europe. Just as the Alps are being uplifted by the pressures of Africa against Europe, Africa once pressed against our east coast, folding the rocks and thrusting them inland to form the Appalachians. North of the Alps is a broad plateau, once a lowland, uplifted by the same pressures that have built the mountains. In the Appalachians a former lowland was likewise uplifted to become the Allegheny and Cumberland plateaus.

Also about 200 million years ago, Greenland was attached to northern Europe, where the Scandinavian Peninsula is today. At the same time, on its western side Greenland was attached to North America, at northern Canada, where Baffin Island is today. Now the Mid-Atlantic Ridge extends northward through Iceland into the North Sea. There as the Mid-Atlantic Ridge gradually widened, Greenland became separated from Scandinavia. A branch of the Mid-Atlantic Ridge also developed on the west side of Greenland, separating that large island from Labrador and Baffin Island. Baffin Island is long and quite slender, directly north of Labrador and separated from Greenland by a narrow stretch of water known as Baffin Bay. Labrador was connected with only the southwest portion of Greenland. But that connection is significant, because formations on the Labrador shore match those of the western shore of Greenland, both in age and structure.

On Iceland, Hekla is the largest volcanic mountain, with a long record of violent eruptions. During the Middle Ages, people were so impressed by the flaming violence of the eruptions, it was assumed that the flaming crater was an opening into hell. Interestingly, Hekla, located near the center of Iceland, along the Mid-Atlantic fissure that bisects the island, has the elongated shape of a high and massive ridge 3 ½ miles long. It is a prominent portion of the Mid-Atlantic Ridge, most of which is out of sight deep within the ocean.

The Atlantic Ocean is in fact spreading as magma rises from the depths at the Mid-Atlantic Ridge. With newer rock being added at the ridge, older rock of the ocean bed is forced apart. It has been found that the ages of rocks composing the ocean bed gradually increase with distance from the ridge.

The gradual spreading from the midocean ridge has brought remarkable changes. Not only have mountains been uplifted along the edges of continents where the pressure of expansion has been applied, but changes of climate have resulted as the continents themselves have moved under pressure. For example, evidence of glaciation in the Sahara Desert is now explained thus: Some 450 million years ago North Africa was close to the South Pole, with the movement of massive glaciers scouring the bedrock below, leaving glacial striations and grooves. The magnetic orientation of elements within the rock indicate the position of the region at that time.

In contrast, the fossil remains of an extinct four-legged reptile, a lizard as large as a modern alligator, have been found in the Antarctic, which indicates a marked change of climate there. Moreover, the remains of such reptiles also found in India and South Africa indicate that those regions were contiguous at one time.

Midocean spreading results in the gradual movement of continents. The large landmasses are made of granite and similar rocks less dense than the basaltic rocks of the ocean beds. So in a sense the continents are floating on the more dense rocks. As rocks of the ocean beds move away from the midocean ridges, the continents move with the ocean beds, gradually drifting away.

Since mountain ranges are ordinarily elevated along coastal regions, where the pressures that lift mountains are applied, how were the Laurentian Mountains built across the middle of North America? More typical are the Appalachians along the East Coast, and in the West, the Cascades and Coast Ranges. Are we to assume that far back in the history of the Earth, the Canadian Shield was the central core of North America, and the Laurentians were elevated along the edge of what then was a continental border? Such a history is doubtful, for it seems that hard rocks encountered at great depths in the central United States are comparable to those of the

Canadian Shield—in fact, a continuation of them. But perhaps those basement rocks in the mid–United States were added after the Laurentians were uplifted. Perhaps it was the pressures of the more southerly basement rocks being added that forced the Laurentians to rise.

The drifting of continents is impelled by the spreading ocean basins. The initial impulse comes from the upwelling magma at the midocean fractures. So the crucial question is what causes the magma to rise at locations such as the Mid-Atlantic Ridge? Although profound questions remain, it seems apparent that the initial impulse comes from a ponderous circulation of somewhat fluid rock under great pressure beneath the Earth's crust. Wherever molten rock breaks through the rigid rocks at the surface, a "hot spot" results, or even a fracture, a midocean rise with volcanoes forming wherever the hot rocks reach the surface. Such circulation has been proposed as an explanation for the Earth's magnetic field. Movement of pliable rock deep within the earth can be likened to the flow of electricity in the coils of an electromagnet. Whatever the initial impulse, some kind of movement in the depths apparently causes molten rock to break through the ocean beds at midocean ridges, and that in turn causes the ocean beds to spread, carrying with them the less dense continental masses in what is called continental drift in the plate tectonic model.

With new rock being added at the central ridges, the ocean beds move outward. Where the dense basaltic rocks of the ocean encounter the edge of a continent, the dense rocks dip down under the lighter crustal rocks of the land. As we have noted, this subduction occurs where the dense rocks of the ocean bed uplift the mountains of Alaska. In such places where the oceanic rocks are moving downward, the subduction tends to create a trench, often carrying sand and other light rocks from the shore downward into it.

Just as volcanic lava adds breadth to an island on the Mid-Atlantic Ridge, so too the outward-moving ocean bed transports oceanic rock to the continents in subduction zones, adding height to the mountains and breadth to the shores. Thus the continents tend to grow as the process continues. Especially noteworthy are other additions to the continents termed *terranes*.

The Addition of Terranes

In California it is readily apparent that a section of coastal land adjoining the San Andreas Fault is gradually separating from the American continent, moving northward in conjunction with rocks of the ocean bed. Except for the resulting earthquakes, the northward movement would be scarcely noticeable, for it is only about two inches a year. Yet if the northward movement continues over a vast period of time, eventually that California coastal strip will merge, violently, with the coast of Canada or Alaska.

Geologists have found that many such mergers have occurred in the distant past. Portions of comparatively light continental rock have drifted northward with the moving ocean basin. Such gradually shifting masses of land are termed *terranes*. It is evident that in the past gradually shifting masses of land have merged with the western side of North America and have become a part of it, making the continent larger.

The evidence indicates that Vancouver Island was originally a tropical island that has moved north to Canada. Another such terrane is in the Mendocino area of California along Highway 101, halfway between San Francisco and the Oregon border. It is mostly marine limestone from the South Pacific. In recent years so many distinctive terranes have been identified that much of the land near the coast seems to have been formed from drifting terranes uniting with the continent. More than 300 foreign terranes have been identified along the West Coast. One of these in the southern portion of California's central valley is itself a hodgepodge of broken bits with different origins, disrupted in transit. Still other terranes have been identified in such places as the Klamath Mountains of southern Oregon and the inland Wind River Mountains of Wyoming.

Sometime in the past, a terrane bearing much gold ore merged with California. A portion of that same terrane broke off and drifted still farther north and became a part of Alaska. Thus it is possible that the gold discovered during the gold rushes in California and Alaska had the same source. Of course, gold ore can be a distinguishing feature, but by no means the only one. A terrane can be distinguished from the adjoining land by being quite unlike the surrounding structures. One may be mostly granite, a type of rock formed deep within the mountains of a landmass. Another may be of a typical coral island, like those of the South Pacific. Any fossils contained also may be different from those in the surrounding rock and quite distinctive. Another feature helpful in distinguishing a terrane from adjoining rocks is the magnetism of those rocks. When a rock hardens, the minerals within it are oriented in the direction of the Earth's magnetism. If that terrane drifts to another location, its magnetism is likely to be different from that of adjoining rocks. As a simple example, a bar magnet once magnetized maintains its polarity even when turned in a different direction. The polarity of rocks formed in the Southern Hemisphere will differ from those of rocks that harden farther north. In addition, the Earth's own magnetism has shifted several times in the distant past, but those changes are known and can be taken into account, helping geologists to determine when the rocks of a terrane were formed, as well as where.

Terranes drifting northward with the moving ocean basin are likely to encounter some portion of the West Coast or Alaska. When the westward drift causes the American continent to override the heavy basaltic rocks of the ocean bed, the lighter rocks of the terrane very likely will not sink but will become attached to the West Coast at the water level. With mountains being uplifted along the coast, the newly attached formations rise with the mountains. Accordingly, many portions of the mountains of Alaska and western Canada are quite different from adjoining rock structures. Commonly, old fault lines, no longer active, separate one portion of a mountain from another. The Wrangell Mountains of southern Alaska are located between the coast and the Canadian border. On the face of a cliff there is basaltic rock that apparently came from a volcanic island somewhere to the south. A stratum of limestone contains tiny marine fossils, likewise indicating the terrane came from an island in the South Seas. In contrast, the adjoining rocks of the cliff are sedimentary, indicating that they were formed on land. When the magnetism of the basaltic terrane was examined, it was found that the terrane had originated far to the south near the equator. In the Arctic a magnetic needle tends to dip toward the North Pole. Farther south at the equator the magnetic lines are parallel with the Earth's surface, and that magnetic orientation indicates that many of the rocks in the Wrangell Mountains of Alaska originated near the equator. In many of the western mountains of Canada, the magnetism of the rocks reveals a similar equatorial origin.

The mountains of Alaska tend to be a jumble of terranes from a variety of sources. In the great Alaskan Range, of which Mount Whitney is a part, the Chulitna Terrane is typical: On the face of a cliff are dark bands of lavas, interspersed with light bands of limestone, both of marine origin. The adjoining rocks are crumpled and massive, containing tropical fossils, indicating that those rocks originated as far away as Southeast Asia. Tropical Asian rocks have been found in the mountains of British Colum bia as well. Such foreign terranes have been found as far inland as the mountains along the Snake River in Idaho.

In 1971 geologists found a terrane in Canada 300 miles from the coast. Those rocks in British Columbia contained fossils known to have been abundant 250 million years ago in an ancient sea that once extended across southern Europe and Asia. It became apparent that the Canadian rocks were formed many millions of years ago and later became attached to the west coast of North America. It was apparent too that the mountains closer to the coast were even younger and contained numerous displaced formations.

Much of the great Alaska Range is no longer close to the shore but does contain foreign terranes. Farther north are the Kuskokwin Mountains. Still farther north is the Brooks Range, well within the Arctic; so it is apparent that Alaska has been built of successive increments, a process that continues today. In northern Canada, the Rocky Mountains and the mountains of the Yukon and the Northwest Territories were apparently developed in a similar way.

Terranes have also been identified along the East Coast. A strip along the coast of the Carolinas contains extinct fossils that are said to indicate an origin in faraway volcanic islands. Such terranes in the East are much more ancient than those of the West, since the West has been much more likely to encounter terranes drifting north with the ocean bed, whereas North America drifts westward to intercept them. But long ago the circumstances were different, as some terranes attached to the East Coast. Some of those additions were quite massive, though also more difficult to identify. One such mass is bounded by a very old fault line circling metropolitan Boston and extending south into Connecticut. Parts of Nova Scotia and Newfoundland may be considered terranes, left behind when the African continent drifted away.

Recently it has been proposed that the landmass that compressed and uplifted the Ouachita Mountains is now in Yucatan as a terrane, withdrawing as the Gulf of Mexico was formed.

It is clear that North America has gone through many profound changes. The spectacular sight of a mountain is perhaps the most telling evidence of this fact.

APPENDICES

Table 1
Estimated Dates of Major Transitions in Geological History

YEARS* AGO	EVENT
4.6 billion	Earth and solar system begin.
3.9 billion	Age of the oldest rocks found in Greenland.
3.8 billion	Life on Earth begins as simple forms in water.
3 billion	Laurentians are uplifted, later reelevated twice.
2.5 billion	Canadian Shield is already intact.
600 million	Beginning of the Paleozoic Era, marked by the first obvious evidence of fossils, the remains of living things.
420 million	Europe and North America merge; the Caledonian Mountains are elevated from eastern Maine and Canada across Greenland and the British Isles and the Scandinavian Peninsula.
300 million	Mountains emerge from the Appalachian trough, extending from eastern Canada and New England to Alabama and beyond.
280 million	Africa merges with the east coast of North America. The Appalachians fully uplifted.
190 million Ocean	Africa withdraws from the east coast of North America; the Atlantic begins to open, also the Gulf of Mexico.
80 million	North America and Europe begin to drift apart. The North Atlantic begins to open between Canada and Europe.
70 million	Rocky Mountains uplifted.
60 million	Greenland and Canada begin to separate.
2 million	The Pleistocene Ice Age begins.
50 thousand	The human beings of today emerge.
10 thousand	Pleistocene Ice Age ends.

*(Ascribing ages in years is merely an approximation, based on the best information available from evidence of meteorites dating back to the beginnings of the solar system, and by radioactive deterioration in rocks on earth. The Ice Age, for example, did not begin or end abruptly, so no exact year can be cited. Mountains, too, are not uplifted abruptly. Accordingly the years indicated are merely reasonable estimates.)

Table 2
Geological Time Scale

ERA	PERIOD	PLANT LIFE	MOUNTAINS	ANIMAL LIFE
CENOZOIC 60 million years	Quaternary Period			Humans dominant
				Mammals and birds
	Tertiary Period	Flowering plants: grass, deciduous trees		
----------	----------	---------- *(R o c k y M o u n t a i n s u p l i f t e d)*		----------
MESOZOIC 135 million years	Cretaceous Period		Appalachians high; Rockies a lowland under water.	
	Jurassic Period	Gingko, cycads, (conifers such as pine, spruce, and fir)		Dinosaurs and other reptiles, insects
	Triassic Period			
----------	----------	---------- *(A p p a l a c h i a n M o u n t a i n s u p l i f t e d)*		----------
PALEOZOIC 350 million years	Permian Period		Present-day mountain and inland areas often under water.	Amphibians
	Pennsylvanian Period	Coal forests: tree ferns, horsetail, rushes, club mosses		
	Mississippian Period			
	Devonian Period			Age of fish
	Silurian Period	Land plants appear		
	Ordovician Period	Simple plants, such as algae, bacteria, and seaweeds		Invertebrate animals in water
	Cambrian Period			
PRECAMBRIAN 4 billion years		No conspicuous fossils, but carbon deposits and imprints of simple forms.		

Table 3
Estimates of Geological Time
(dates in millions of years ago)

ERAS	PERIODS		EPOCHS
CENOZOIC 65–Present		**Quaternary** 2–Present	**Holocene** (Recent) 0.01–Present
			Pleistocene (Ice Age) 2–0.01
		Neogene or Late Tertiary 24.6–2	**Pliocene** 5–2
MESOZOIC 248–65		**Paleogene or Early Tertiary** 65–24.6	**Miocene** 24.6–5
		Cretaceous 144–65	**Oligocene** 38–24.6
			Eocene 55–38
		Jurassic 213–144	**Paleocene** 65–55
PALEOZOIC 590–248		**Triassic** 248–213	
		Permian 286–248	
		Carboniferous 360–286	
		Devonian 408–360	
		Silurian 440–408	
		Ordovician 505–440	
		Cambrian 590–505	

**Table 4
Some Common Rocks**

Igneous	Sedimentary	Metamorphic
pegmatite	conglomerate	gneiss
granite gabbro	sandstone	quartzite
felsite basalt (trap)	shale	slate, phyllite, schist
	limestone	marble
	chert	

CHART OF THE IGNEOUS ROCKS

Igneous rocks are massive. They are identified by their color, their texture, and their minerals.

Color

Rocks light in color and density. (Acidic: rich in silica and orthoclase feldspar).

Rocks that are dark and heavy. (Basic: rich in calcium, iron, and magnesium compounds).

Igneous rocks

Texture						
coarse	pegmatite					
	granite	syenite	quartz-diorite	diorite	gabbro	peridotite
	rhyolite (felsite)	trachyte (felsite)	dacite	andesite	basalt	limburgite
smooth	obsidian					

Minerals

orthoclase, quartz, etc.	no quartz, but orthoclase etc.	plagioclase, biotite, hornblend, with quartz	plagioclase, biotite, hornblend, but no quartz	plagioclase, pyroxene, etc.	hornblend, pyroxene, etc. but no feldspar

Table 5
Relationships of Common Rocks

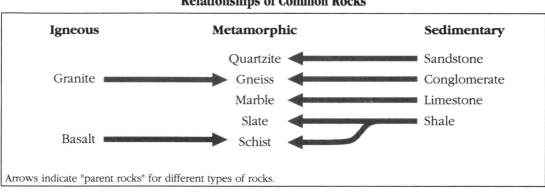

Arrows indicate "parent rocks" for different types of rocks.

INDEX

This index is arranged alphabetically leter-by-letter.
Major topics are indicated by **boldface** page numbers;
illustrations by *italic* page numbers; and table by *"t."*

A

Aberdeen (Washington) 26
abrasives 95
Acadia National Park vii
Acadian Disturbance 79
Acadian Mountains 34, 36
acids 152, 168
Adams, Mount 21, 22, 116
Adirondack Mountains 34, 109, 132, 166–169
Africa 58, 79, 137, 139, 161, 170, 175
Agassiz, Louis 96
Alabama 82, 140, 175
Alaska
  Aniakchak National Monument 11
  Appalachian uplift 59
  earthquakes 2–3
  glaciers *87, 92, 106,* 117
  "Inside Passage" 171
  Katmai eruption 10–11
  Lake Clark National Park and Reserve 11
  lava fields 40
  Mount Redoubt 10
  Rocky Mountains uplift 37
  terranes 178, 179–180
  valley trains 110
  volcanoes 10
  Wrangell Mountains 179
Alaska, Gulf of 5
Alaska Mountain Range 3–6, 59, 179–180
Alaskan Highway 171
Albany (New York) 110, 123, 127, 133
Aleutian Islands 3, 10, 40
algae 4, 34, 50, *158,* 166, 170
Algoman Revolution 167
Allegheny Mountains viii, 73, 133, 134
Allegheny Plateau 73, 110, 122, 123, 125, 128, 132, 175
Allegheny River 112, 122
Alps 31, 59, 96, 114, 175

Altar of Sacrifices 51
altered basalt 150
Amarillo Mountains 35, 80–81
American Museum of Natural History (New York City) 162, 166
American Revolution 104, 138
amethyst 156
Anchorage (Alaska) 2–3, 10, 110
Andes 31
andesite 186*t*
Androscoggin River 64
Aniakchak National Monument 11
Antarctica 92, 161, 176
anthracite 35
anticlines 38, 84
apatite 155
Appalachian Mountains
  Catskill Delta 132
  earthquake evidence vi
  erosion x, **63–75,** 119, 121, 140, 168
  "Folded Appalachians" 56
  in geological history 32–34, 36, 175
  glacial evidence 92, 112
  outline of rock structure in *63*
  plateaus **123–137**
  thrust faults 54
  Trans-Canada Highway through ix
  uplift **53–85,** 157
  volcanic activity 55–57, **60–63**
Appalachian Trail 133
Arbuckle Mountains 35, 80
arches 47, 51
Arches National Park 50, 51
Arctic 179
arête 115
Arethusa Falls 91
Arkansas
  Ouchita Mountains 79–85

Ozarks viii
Arkansas River 82, 83, 85, 120
Arkansas Valley 84
Arnold Arboretum (Massachusetts) 107
Ascension Islands 174
Asheville (North Carolina) 78
Astoria (Oregon) 13, 24
Athabasca Glacier *13,* 117
Athabasca River 117
Atlantic City (New Jersey) 138
Atlantic Coastal Plain 76, 134, 137–141
Atlantic Hill 62
Atlantic Ocean 57–58, 81, 137, 174, 176
Atlas Mountains 59, 75, 79
augite 156
avalanches 21
Azores 174

B

"Badlands" *122*
Baffin Island 175
Baileyville (Connecticut) 162
Baja California 48
Baker, Mount viii, 10, 21, 116
Bald Mountain 39
balite *146*
Banff National Park 117
barrier beaches 138–139
barrier islands 138
Bartlett Boulder 93
basalt 11, 14, *56,* 60, 67, 143, 145, 150, 176–177, 179, 186*t,* 187*t*
basaltic lava *8,* 18, 42, 61
Batchlor Butte 18
batholiths **39–41,** 79
Baxter State Park 65
beaches
  barrier beaches 138–139
  Cannon Beach 24
  erosion 138–139

igneous rocks 143
Nantasket Beach 62, 104
outwash plain 100
pebbles/stones *83,* 151
terminal moraines 98
Beacon Hill 104
Beacon Street (Boston, Mass.) 66–67
Bearhat Mountain 114
bedrock 37, 90, 93, *94, 95,* 99, 151, 153
Bellingham (Washington) viii, 116, 163
"Belted Plains" 140
Bemis Brook (New Hampshire) 91
Berlin (Connecticut) 101
Bicentennial Memorial (Washington, D.C.) vii
Big Bone Lick State Park (Kentucky) 163
Big Muddy River 120
birch trees 91, 133
Black Belt 140
Black Hills viii, 167, 169
black lava 62
Block Island 97
"block mountains" 42
Bluefield (West Virginia) viii, 133, 160, 165
Blue Glacier 116
Blue Hill 64
Blue Mountains 17, 73, 130
Blue Ridge Mountains 74, **75–79,** 133, *136*
Blue Ridge Parkway vii
Bonaparte, Napoleon *see* Napoleon Bonaparte
Bonneville Dam 22
Boston (Massachusetts)
  conglomerate *57–58,* 66–67
  drumlins 104–105
  glacial evidence 62, *94,* 102
  terranes 180
  volcanic activity 56, 67
Boston Basin 59, 62, 67, 74, 103, 105

Boston Harbor 102
Boston Mountains 84
boulders 70, *89, 90,* 93, 96–99, 102–104, 112, 119, 124, 150–152
Brazos River 140
breccia 18, 154
Breeds Hill 104
Bremerton (Washington) 22
bricks 101
Bridal Veil Falls 22, 91
Bridge of the Gods 22
Bristol (Connecticut) 75
British Columbia (Canada) 13, 22, 117
British Isles 175, 183*t*
Broken Top (Oregon) 18
brontosaurus 162
Bronx Zoo (New York City) 99
Brookhaven National Laboratory (New York) 97
Brookline (Massachusetts) 104
Brooklyn (New York City borough) 97
Brooks Range 180
Bryce Canyon National Park 50, *51,* 152
Buffalo (New York) 110, 128
Bunker Hill 104
Burlington (Vermont) 54
Buzzard's Bay (Massachusetts) 97, 99

C

Cadillac Mountain vii
calcite 150, 155, 156
calderas and craters
    Alaskan sites 10–11
    Mammoth Lakes 42–43
    Medicine Lake 19
    Mono Lake 43
    Mount Rainier 20
    Mount Saint Helens 8–9, 12
    Newberry volcano 17–18
    Sunset Crater 49
    Yellowstone Park 39
Caledonian Mountains 183*t*
Calgary (Canada) 170
California *see also* San Andreas Fault
    continental drift vii
    fault lines 48
    glaciers 90
    Lava Beds National Monument 18
    lava fields 12, 18–19
    in Native American folklore vi
    terraces 139
    terranes 177–180
California, Gulf of 2, 45, 48

Cambrian Period 34, 157
camels 48
Canada *see also* Canadian Shield
    batholiths 39
    geological milestones 183*t*
    glaciers 92, 96, 111, 117
    lava fields 12
    Watertown Lakes National Park ix
Canadian Shield ix, x, 34, 81, 169, 170, 176–177, 183*t*
Cannon Beach 24
Canyonlands National Park 50
Cape Ann (Massachusetts) 102, 105
Cape Breton Island ix
Cape Cod (Massachusetts) 97–100, 105, 112, 139
Cape Cod Bay 100
Cape Flattery (Washington) 23
Cape Hatteras (North Carolina) 138
Capitol Reef National Park 50
carbon 34, 35, 37, 156, 157, 168, 184*t*
carbon dioxide 31–32, 72, 135
carbonic acid 72, 135
Carboniferous Period 35, 185*t*
Carlsbad Caverns 136
Carmel, Mount 60, 100
Cascade Mountains *9*
    climate 28–30
    in folklore v
    fossils 163–164
    glaciers 88, *114,* 115
    rainfall 25–26
    relative youth of 32–34
    uplift 31, 164
    volcanic activity 7, 10, 12, 55
Catskill Delta 127, 128, 130, 132
Catskill Mountains 34, 110, *123,* 164
Catskill Plateau 124–125
caves and caverns 18, 107, 109, 135, 136, 140
Cayuga Lake 125–126
Cedar Breaks National Monument 50, 51
Cenozoic Era 33, 50, 184*t*, 185*t*
Central America 11–12
Central Park (New York City) 99, 149
Champlain, Lake *53,* 54, 168
Charles River 102
chert 147
Chesapeake Bay 137, 138

Cheshire (Connecticut) 100
Cheyenne (Wyoming) 30
Cheyenne River 120
Chief Mountain vi
China 6, 15
chlorite schist 150
Chulitna Terrane 179
cinder cones 18, 19, 49
citrus groves 139
Clark Fork River 15
clay
    in Boston area 103, 104
    in Catskill Delta 127
    in Connecticut Valley 101
    in early Appalachians 60, 72, 168
    feldspar converted to 143
    on Gulf Coastal Plain 140
    along Lake Erie 111
    in Puget Sound 22
    shale and 152, 153, 159
    in terminal moraines 97, 112
Clear Lake 18
Clements Mountain 114
cliff dwellings 52
cliffs 48, 52, 91, 100, 110, 138, 179
climate 28–32
Cloverdale (California) 47
coal 31, 35, 37, 54, 159–160, 164, 165
Coastal Mountain Range 31, 39, 48
cobalt 169
Coleman Glacier 116
Colombia 11–12, 81
Colorado vi, 38
Colorado Plateau 31, 38, 49, 50, 162, 164
Colorado River 38, 48
Columbia ice fields 13, 117
Columbia River 6, 7, 13–14, 15, 24, 29, 163
Columbia River Highway 22
Columbus (Ohio) 112
columnar jointing vii, 42
Commonwealth Avenue (Boston, Mass.) 67
composite volcanoes 63
"concoidal fracture" 156
Coney Island 98
conglomerate
    in Boston area *57, 58,* 66–67
    in Cumberland Mountains 55, 134
    and fossils 159
    gneiss converted from 148, 187*t*
    identification of 154
    in Natural Bridge State Park 133

Roxbury conglomerate 59
    as sedimentary rock 147
    in Shawangunk Mountain 129–130
    in Sugarloaf Mountains 69
Connecticut River 67–68, 76, 101
Connecticut Valley vi, 33, 60, 61, 69, 74, 75, 100, 101, 109, *161,* 162
contact metamorphism 159
continental divide 15, 39
continental drift *see* plate tectonics
continental glacier 113
continental shelf 75, 78, 137
convection currents 81
Conway (New Hampshire) 94
Cook Inlet (Alaska) 10
copper 169
coral 158, 178
Cordova (Alaska) 3, 5
Cornell University 125, 139
corundum 155
coulees 15
Cowhorn Mountain 18
Cowlitz River 116
cranberry bogs 105
Crater Lake vi, 12, *17, 24,* 43
craters *see* calderas and craters
Craters of the Moon National Monument vi, 16, 40, 166
Crawford Notch (New Hampshire) 91
Crescent City (California) 5–6
Crescent Lake 23
Cretaceous Period 184*t*, 185*t*
crevasse 105–106, 107
crustal disturbances 16, 80
crystalline rocks 80
crystals 60–61, 92, 145, 148–149, 152–154
Cuba 82
Cumberland Gap 55
Cumberland Mountains 55, 134
Cumberland Plateau 122, 134, *135,* 136, 175
Cumberland River 122, 136

D

dacite 12, 61, 186*t*
dams 15, 22, 100, 121
Dawson Creek (Canada) 171
Death Valley 30, 42, 49
Delaware River 130
Delaware Water Gap 74
deltas 120, 124, 127, 132, 141

density 154–155
Denver (Colorado) vii, 30, 39, *120,* 121
depressions 42, 43, 53, 74
Deschutes National Forest 17
Desert State Park 48
Devil's Postpile 42, *44*
Devil's Tower vi
Devonian Period 34, 128–129, 184*t,* 185*t*
diamonds 155
dikes 61, 67
Dinosaur National Monument 162
dinosaurs vi, 15, 33, 50, 67–68, *68–69,* 70, 159, 162
Dinosaur State Park 162
diorite 186*t*
dolomite limestone *53,* 54, 128, *130*
Dougherty Plains 140
drainage patterns 64
Driskill Mountain 141
drowned valleys 23
drumlins 62, 96, 103, 104–105, 108, 109–110, 116
Duluth (Minnesota) 34, 169

E

earthquakes
   in Alaska 2–4, 5
   in California *see* San Andreas Fault
   causes of 4
   global devastation caused by 6–7
   and joint formation 150
   in Mississippi Valley 82
   and mountain building vi, ix, 32, 43–44
   volcanoes and 10
Eastham (Massachusetts) 99
East Harwich (Massachusetts) 100
East Orleans (Massachusetts) 100
East River Mountain viii
ecosystems 9
El Centro (California) 48
El Chichon (Mexico) 12
electricity 15, 121, 177
elephants 104, 137
Ellensburg (Washington) 163
embayment 139, 141
entrenched meander 71
Eocene Epoch 185*t*
Erie, Lake 110, 111, 112
erosion
   of Allegheny Mountains 133
   of Appalachian Plateau 121
   of Appalachians 59, **63–75,** 119, 160
   of beaches 138–139
   of Catskills 123
   of Colorado Plateau 50–51
   of Cumberland Plateau 135
   and glaciers 110
   of high plains 121
   and igneous rocks 144–145
   of Laurentians 167
   and metamorphic rocks 150
   of Ozark Plateau 123
   of Rockies *38*
   and sedimentary rocks 147
   of Taconic Mountains 133
   of Tetons 38
   and "trap" ridges 61
   of Uintas 38
   of Wasatch Range 42
erratics 93, *93*
eskers **107–109**
Etna, Mount 59
Eurasia 79
evaporation 25
Everglades 139
exfoliation *151,* 152

F

Fall Line 137
farming 29, 83, 121
Farmington River 100, 101
fault lines
   in Boston area 62
   in California 45–47 *see also* San Andreas Fault
   in Coastal Plain 139
   glaciers and 116
   in Inyo National Forest *43*
   Lake Champlain 168
   mountain building and vi, 32, 78
   in Mount Tom Reservation 68
   in New York State 111
   in Oklahoma vii
   Pine Mountain exposure 134
   terranes 179, 180
   thrust faults 66–67, 74, 133
   trap ridges 101
   in Yucatan Peninsula 81
feldspar 143, *146,* 155
felsite 8, 63, 145, *146,* 152, 153–154, 156, 186*t*
Finger Lakes 110
fir trees 28–29, 64, 91, 133
fish and fishing 34, 137, 159
Fisher's Island 98
Flagstaff (Arizona) 49
Flatwoods 140
flintlike chert 84

floods 15, 121, 122, 123
Florence (Kentucky) 163
Florida 139
fluorite 155
flying lizard 166
"Folded Appalachians" *54,* 56, 76, 79, 134
folding 55, 56, 66–67, *71,* 72, 83, 84, 153, 154, 175
foliation 149, 153
"fool's gold" *see* pyrite
Fordham gneiss 34
Forks (Washington) 23
fossils
   in Antarctica 176
   in Boston area 104
   Cambrian Period 34
   Canadian Shield devoid of 170
   in Cascade Range 163–164
   at Clear Lake 18
   in coal mines 159–160
   on Coastal Plain 137
   in Connecticut Valley 162
   of dinosaurs 159, 162
   formation of **157–160**
   in Grand Canyon region 50–51
   of plants 159
   in Precambrian rocks 49–50
   and rock identification 154
   in sedimentary rocks 157–160
   in shale 159
   significance of **161–162**
   sites **162–166**
   in terranes 178–179, 180
   of trees 15, 34, 123, *124,* 164, 165
   in Washington State 163
"fracture" 156
French and Indian War ix
Fresh Pond 102
fur trade 24

G

gabbro 144, *145,* 186*t*
Garden Wall (Glacier Park, Mont.) 115
Garibaldi, Mount 22
Gaspé Peninsula 78
Genesee Gorge 35, 129
Genesee River 110, 127
George, Lake 168
Georgia vii, 139
geysers 10, 39, 47
giant club moss *165*
giants v
Ginkgo State Park (Washington) 15, 163
ginkgo trees 15, 163
glacial dams 100

glacial stones 94, 96, 151
glacial till 90, 103, 117
Glacier National Park vi, ix, 37, 91, *113,* 114, *115,* 165
Glacier Peak 22
glaciers
   Adirondacks shaped by 109
   in Alaska 92, *106*
   Appalachians shaped by 92
   Athabasca Glacier *13*
   boulders and 93
   in Canada x, 92, 96, 117, 170, 171
   Cascades shaped by 115
   Catskills shaped by 110
   eskers **107–109**
   formation of 42
   fossils 165
   Grinnell Glacier 166
   hanging glaciers 116
   lakes 98, 101, 112, *114*
   in Maine 139
   in the Midwest **112–113**
   in Montana vi
   mountain building and **87–119**
   Mount Baker shaped by viii
   Mount Olympus shaped by 23
   Mount Shuksan shaped by 21
   in New England 62, **91–109**
   in New York State **109–112**
   Nisqually Glacier *88,* 89
   in Oregon 117
   Portage Glacier *87*
   Puget Sound 22
   recession of 116
   terminal moraines **96–99**
   in Washington State 116
   waterfalls 102
   in the West **113–117**
Glass Mountain 19, *20*
Glen Falls 168
Gloucester (Massachusetts) 102
gneiss 34, 94, 147–150, 153, 169, 187*t*
Goat Island (New York) 128
gold 154, 169, 178
Golden Gate Bridge (San Francisco, Calif.) 47
gorges vi, 13, 110, 111, *125,* 126, 127, *128,* 129, *130*
Grand Canyon 16, 38, 47, 49, 50, 162, 164, 167
Grand Coulee 15
Grand River 120

Grand Teton Mountains 15, 38
granite 186t, 187t
    in Adirondacks 168
    in Alaska Mountain Range 4
    in Appalachians 62
    in bicentennial memorial vii
    in Black Hills 169
    composition of 143, 155, 156
    domes 45, 150, 152
    erratics 94
    fossils in 159
    gabbro contrasted with 144, 145
    gneiss compared to 147–148
    in Green Mountains 144
    identification of 154
    at Joshua National Monument 152
    in large landmasses 176
    in Mount Katahdin 65
    as "Old Appalachia" evidence 78
    on Ozark Plateau 83
    pegmatite/felsite contrasted with 146
    quartz eroded from 164
    in San Bernardino Mountains 49
    in Sierra Nevada 42
    in terranes 178
    in Tetons 38
    weathering of 150
    in White Mountains 34, 64, 79
Granite Mountain vii
granitoid 144–145, 150, 168
graphite 168
graptolites 159
gravel 95, 103, 107, 108, 124, 130
Grays Harbor 6
Great Basin 42
Great Central Valley 47
Great Dismal Swamp 138
Great Falls (Montana) 114
Great Lakes 132, 167
Great Plains vi, 30, 39, 81, 119–123, 122, 169, 170
Great Salt Lake 37, 41, 131
Great Smoky Mountains 78, 133
Great Valley 72, 134
Great White Throne 51
Greenland 92, 96, 170, 174, 175, 183t
Green Mountains vii, 54, 144
Grenville System 167
Grinnell Glacier 166
ground moraine 90

Gulf Coastal Plain 80, 82, 140
gypsum 155

H

Half Dome 44
hanging glaciers 116
Hanging Hills 60
hanging valley 91
Harrisburg (Pennsylvania) 73
Hartford (Connecticut) 162
Haverhill (Massachusetts) 102
Hawaii
    igneous rocks 143
    lava fields 13
    volcanoes 8, 11
Hawk's Nest (West Virginia) viii
Hekla Mountain 175–176
Hell's Canyon 16
hemlocks 28–29, 91
Hempstead Plain 97
"high plains" 121
Himalayas 6, 13, 31, 59
Hingham Bay 104
Hoh River 23
Holbrook (Arizona) 49
Holocene Epoch 185t
Holyoke Range (Massachusetts) 60, 68
Homer (Alaska) 5
Hood, Mount viii, 10, 22, 117
Hopis 49
horizontal strata 134
hornblende 143, 148, 150, 156
hornfel 159
Horn Pond 102
horns 114
"hot spot" 177
hot springs 39, 83
Hudson Bay 92
Hudson River 61, 159, 166
Hudson Valley 123, 129, 132, 149
Hull (Massachusetts) 104
humidity 25–26
humus 140, 147
Huron, Lake 170
Hurricane Ridge 23, 116

I

Ice Age
    Chesapeake Bay formation 138
    and Columbia River 15
    conditions before 31
    effects of 31
    geological record of x
    and Great Salt Lake 41
    La Brea Tar Pit fossils 48, 163
    ongoing in Montana vi
    and Puget Sound 22

volcanic activity during 22
Icefield Parkway 117
Iceland 173–174, 175–176
Idaho 15–16, 30, 39, 40
igneous rocks 74, 75, 143–147, 152, 153, 159, 169, 170, 186t, 187t
Imperial Valley 2, 48
index fossils 162
India 6, 59
Indiana 35
industry 102
"Inside Passage" (Alaska) 171
Inyo National Forest 43
iron 60, 169
iron oxide 72, 156
iron rust 127, 147
irrigation 29, 48, 121
Italy 59
Ithaca (New York) 110, 125–126, 127, 132

J

Jamaica Plain 104
Jamaica Pond 104, 107
James River 137–138
Japan 15
Jasper (Canada) ix
Jasper National Park 117
Jefferson, Mount 18
Jensen (Utah) 163
Job's Pond 109
Johnstown flood (1889) 122
joints (in rocks) 150–151
Jones Beach (New York) 98
Joshua National Monument 152
Joshua trees 48
Juan de Fuca, Strait of 6, 22, 23
Jurassic Period 15, 162, 163, 184t, 185t

K

kames 96, 107, 108, 109
Kansas 120
Katahdin, Mount 64, 65, 79, 133
Katmai National Park 10
Kenai Peninsula 5
Kentucky 35, 135, 165, 174
kettle holes 105, 109
Kilauea volcano 11
Killarney Revolution 167
King River 84
King's Canyon National Park 45, 46, 150
Kirkjufell (Iceland) 173
Kittatiny Mountain 130
Klamath Mountains 46, 47, 178
Kodiak Island (Alaska) 4
Kuskokwim Mountains 180

L

Labrador (Canada) 167, 170, 175
La Brea Tar Pits (Los Angeles, Calif.) 48, 163
lagoon 139
Laguna Mountains 48
Lake Clark National Park and Reserve 11
lakes 101, 112, 114, 131, 132 see also specific lakes (e.g., Superior, Lake)
Lamentation Mountain 109
Landscape Arch 51
landslides 3, 5, 6
Lassen, Mount 19
lateral moraines 117
Laurentian Mountains 167–170, 176–177, 183t
lava
    conglomerate contrasted with 154
    fields 12–19, 40, 46, 60
    fossil imprints in 159, 164
    igneous rocks formed from 143, 145
    jointing 150
    mountain building and 32, 168
    sites
        Appalachians 60–63
        Cascade Mountains 55
        Colorado Plateau 50
        Hawaii 11
        Iceland 174
        Mount Garibaldi 22
        Mount Jefferson 18
        Rocky Mountains 40, 40–41
        Sierra Nevada 42
    sources
        midocean ridges 173–177
        Mount Saint Helens 7–9
        Newberry volcano 17
        Sunset Crater 49
    tunnels 18
Lava Beds National Monument 18
Lavalands 17
Lawrence (Massachusetts) 102
Letchworth State Park (New York) 110, 127, 128, 132
level lines 42
Lewis and Clark Expedition 24
Lewis Overthrust 37
Lexington (Kentucky) 133
Lexington (Massachusetts) 102

limestone
  in bicentennial memorial vii
  in Black Hills 169
  caverns 18
  at Cedar Breaks National Monument 51
  in concrete 147
  dolomite limestone *53*, 54
  in Florida 139
  fossils in 158–160
  identification of 152, 154
  at Mammoth Cave 136
  marble converted from 79, 150, 187*t*
  marine limestone 178
  Midwestern formations 35, 135
  across New York State 129
  at Niagara Falls 111, 128
  in Ontario 131
  in Ozarks 83–84
  in Shenandoah Valley 77
  at Timpanogos Cave 50
  vulnerability to acid 168
  in western New England 74
Ling's Canyon National Park 39
Little Falls 111
Little Missouri River 120, 121
Little Rock (Arkansas) 82, 83
loam 147
loess 147
Logan Pass 114–115
Long Beach (New York) 98
Long Island (New York) 97, 112
Long Island Sound 60, 98, 100, 101
Long's Peak (Colorado) 39
Los Angeles (California) 2, 45, 152, 163
Louisiana 141
Lowell (Massachusetts) 101, 102
Lower California *see* Baja California
lowland shank 160
Lyman Hill (Brookline, Mass.) 104

M

Madison Boulder 93–94
magma *8*, 10, 44, 143–147, 169, 176–177
magnetism 177, 178–179
Magnus, Albertus v
Maiden Peak 18
Maine 91, 109, 137, 139, 183*t*

Maine, Gulf of 137
Mammoth Cave 35, 136
Mammoth Lakes 42–43, 44
mammoths 48, 104
Mansfield, Mount 95
maples 91
marble 79, 150, 152, 154, 159, 187*t*
Marconi, Guglielmo 99
marine climate 24, 28
marine limestone 178
marl 140, 147
marshland 139
Martha's Vineyard (Massachusetts) 97
Massachusetts Bay 57–58
mastodons 48, 104, 163
Matterhorn 114
Mazama, Mount vi
McKenzie River 18
McKinley, Mount 3, 5, 40, 110, 117
Medicine Lake 19
Mediterranean Sea 175
meltwater 106, 107, 109, 119, 151
Mendocino (California) 46, 178
Mendocino Fault 46
Meriden (Connecticut) 109, 162
Merrimac River 101, 102
Mesabi Range 169
Mesa Verde National Park 52
Mesozoic Era x, 15, 33, 50, 163, 184*t*, 185*t*
metamorphic rocks 64–65, 75, 143, **147–150**, 152–153, 159, 168, 169, 186*t*, 187*t*
Mexico 11–12
Mexico, Gulf of vi, 30, 79, 81, 82, 85, 120, 121, 140
Mexico City (Mexico) 6–7
Miami (Florida) 30, 138
mica 92, 143, *146*, 149–150, 156
Michigan, Lake 110
Mid-Atlantic Ridge 174–177
midocean ridges **173–177**
Mill River 100, 101
minerals v, 15, 18, 32, 41, 49, 143–146, 154–155, 166, 178
mining 132, 159–160, 164, 169
Miocene Epoch 185*t*
missionaries 24
Mississippi 79–85, 82
Mississippian Period 35, 184*t*
Mississippi Delta 83, 127
Mississippi River 120, 121, 127, 140
Mississippi Valley 82, 141, 147

Missouri (U.S. battleship) 22
Missouri River 84, 92, 119–120
Mitchell, Mount 78, 150
Mohawk River 111, 132
Mohawk Valley 111, 121, 129, 132, 168
Mohs scale 155
Mojave Desert 30, 42, 48–49
molten rock 10, 12, 18, 55, 59, 60, 67, 100, 143, 145, 156, 177
Monadnock, Mount 63–64, *64*
monadnocks 64, 78
Mono Lake 43
Monomy Island (Massachusetts) 100
Monongahela River 112, 122
Montague Island (Alaska) 4
Montana vi, ix
Montauk Point 97
Monterey, Bay of 47
Montreal (Canada) ix
moraines 96
Morristown (New Jersey) 98
Mossyrock (Washington) 25
mountain ash 133
Mountain Parkway 133
mud 120, 121, 159
  cracks 160, 165
  pots 10, 39
Muir Woods National Monument 47
Multnomah Falls 22
Mystic Lakes 102
Mystic River 102

N

Nantasket Beach 62, 104
Nantucket (Massachusetts) 97
Nantucket Sound 100
Naples (New York) 164
Napoleon Bonaparte 174
Narragansett Bay 99
Nashua (New Hampshire) 101
Nashville (Tennessee) 136
national parks viii, 24, 44–45
Native Americans 23, 49, 52
Natural Bridge State Park 50, 133
Navajos 52
Neah Bay 23
Nebraska 120
Nebraska River 120
Neogene Period 185*t*
Nevada 12, 19
Newberry volcano 17
New Britain (Connecticut) 75, 76, 101

New Brunswick (Canada) 74, 79
New England, glacial geology of **91–109**
Newfoundland (Canada) 175, 180
New Haven (Connecticut) 100
New Madrid earthquakes 82
New Mexico 38
New Orleans (Louisiana) 120, 127
New River *70*, 71
Newton (Massachusetts) 61, 108–109
New York City 15, 34, 99, 149, 162 *see also* Brooklyn; Staten Island
New York State 78, **109–112**, 132
New York State Museum (Albany, N.Y.) 164
Niagara Escarpment 110
Niagara Falls 35, 110, 111, 128, *129*
Niagara gorge 110, *130*
nickel 169
Nisqually Glacier *88*, 89, 116
Norfolk (Virginia) 138
normal faults 37–38
North Atlantic Ocean 175
North Carolina 133, 138
North Dakota 121
North Sea 79, 175
North Truro (Massachusetts) 99
Northwest Territories (Canada) 180
"notches" 74
Nova Scotia (Canada) ix, 74, 79, 175, 180

O

Oakland (California) 1–2
oaks 91
obsidian 19, 145–146, 186*t*
ocean bed
  midocean ridges 173–177
  mountain building 4–6
  volcanic activity 10, 11
Odell Butte (Oregon) 18
Ogden (Utah) 37
Ohio 30, 122, 165
Ohio River 92, 112, 122
oil 31, 48, 161–162
Okeechobee, Lake 139
Okefenokee Swamp 139
Oklahoma vii, 35, 79–85, 80
"Old Appalachia" 78–79
Oligocene Epoch 185*t*
Olympia (Washington) 22
Olympic Mountains v, 23, 25–26, 28, 116
Olympic National Park 22

Olympus, Mount 23
Oneida, Lake 111
Onondaga (New York) 132
Ontario (Canada) 131
Ontario, Lake 109, 110, 127, 129
Ordovician Period 184*t*, 185*t*
Oregon
  Cascades as dividing line 28
  glaciers 117
  lava fields 16
  Mount Hood viii, 22
  Three Sisters 18
Oregon Caves National Monument 18
Oregon Dunes National Recreation Area 24
"Oregon mist" 25
ores 169–170
Orleans (Massachusetts) 97
Osage River 84
Oswego (New York) 110
Ouachita Mountains 35, **79–85**, *80*, 140–141, 180
Ouachita National Forest 84
Ouachita River 84
Outer Banks (North Carolina) 138
outwash plain 97, 99, 100, 101, 103, 104, 106, 109, 112
Owens Valley 42
oxygen 31, 127
Ozark Plateau **79–85**, 123
Ozarks viii, 147

P

Pacific Ocean 13, 23, 28, 59
Painted Desert 49, 164
Paleocene Epoch 185*t*
Paleozoic Era 33–36, 50, 53, 78, 79, 81, 129, 164, 183*t*, 184*t*, 185*t*
Palisades 61
Pangaea 79, 81
parallel lines 99
Parker Hill 104
Pecos River 120
pegmatite 145, *146, 148*, 155, 186*t*
Pend Oreille Lake 15
peninsulas 3, 10, 67, 99, 175
Pennsylvania viii, 72–73
Pennsylvanian Period 35, 184*t*
Pennsylvania Turnpike 73
Perícutin (Mexico) 12
peridotite 186*t*
Permian Basin 81
Permian Period 184*t*, 185*t*
Permian sediments 82
Petrified Forest National Park 15, 49, 159, 164
phyllites 150
Piedmont Range 133, 137, 143

Piedmont Rocks **75–79**, *76*
Pilgrim Heights (Massachusetts) 99
Pine Mountains 54–55
pine trees 29, 49, 84
Pinnacle Rocks State Park (West Virginia) *73*, 133
Pinnacles National Monument 47
Pittsburgh (Pennsylvania) 112, 122
Plainfield (New Jersey) 98
plains *see specific plains* (e.g., Atlantic Coastal Plain)
Plainville (Connecticut) 101
plants *see* fossils; vegetation
plateaus *see specific plateau* (e.g., Allegheny Plateau)
plate tectonics 31, **57–58**, 75, 79, 81, 83, 85, 161, 170, 177
Platte River 120
Pleasant Bay 99–100
Pleiades vii
Pleistocene Epoch 185*t*
Pliny v
Pliocene Epoch 185*t*
Pocahontas Exhibition Mine 160, 165
Pocono Mountains viii, 130
Point Reyes National Seashore (California) 2, 6, 47
Portage Glacier *87*
Port Angeles (Washington) 116
Portland (Connecticut) 109
Portland (Maine) 91
Portland (Oregon) viii, 7, 22, 117
potassium 157
Potomac River 74, *77,* 137–138
Precambrian Period 34, 49–50, 166, 184*t*
Presidential Range 92
Prospect Point (New York) 128
Provincetown (Massachusetts) 99
"pudding stone" 57
Puget Sound v, viii, 22–23, 47, 163
pulverized rock 117
pumice vi, 7–9, 10, 12, 18
Pumice Butte (Oregon) 18
pyrite *146,* 154
Pythagoras v

Q

quartz 12, 49, 143, *146, 147,* 153, 154, 155, 156, 164, 186*t*

quartzite 78, 130, 150, 153–154, 168
Quaternary Period 184*t*, 185*t*
Quebec (Canada) ix, 170
Quilcene (Washington) 25, 27
Quinnipiac (Connecticut) 101

R

radiation 156
radio 99
radioactivity 156–157, 170
radium 157
radon 157
railroads 92, 110, 117
Rainbow Bridge National Monument 50
rainfall 23, 25–26, 28, 30, 121, *161*
rain forests 23, 28
Rainier, Mount viii, 20–21, *21,* 24, *88,* 116
rain shadow 25–26, 29, 42
rapids 14, 137
Rappahannock River 137
ravines 42, 62, 68–69
recessional moraines *90,* 105, 116
recessions 116
Redoubt, Mount 10
Redoubt Number Ten 138
Red River 121
red sandstone *123,* 124
Redwood National Park 47
redwoods 47
reefs 158
Regina (Canada) 170
reptiles 166, 176
resorts viii, ix
Retsof (New York) 132
Reynolds Mountain 114
Rhode Island Sound 99
rhyolite 186*t*
rift valley 174
Rio Grande 120
ripple marks 160, 165
Riverside (California) 152
Riverside Drive (New York City) 99
Robert Moses Parkway 110
robins 30
Rochester (New York) 109, 110, 127, 129, 132
rock flour 119
Rockport (Massachusetts) 102
rocks *see specific types* (e.g., igneous rocks)
Rocky Hill (Connecticut) 101
Rocky Mountain National Park 39
Rocky Mountains
  age x, 81, 157, 183*t*
  batholiths 39–41

as Columbia River source 13
erosion *38*
fossils 159
lava flows *40,* 40–41
rainfall patterns 30
sedimentation 119–120, 140
terranes 180
uplift 31, 33–34, **37–41**, 164
Rosendale (New York) 130
Roxbury conglomerate 59
Rushmore, Mount viii

S

saber-toothed tigers 48
Saco Lake 92
Saco River 91
sagebrush 16
Sahara Desert 176
Saint Francois Mountains 83
Saint Helena 174
Saint Helens, Mount ix, 6, 7–9, *8,* 12, 20, 22, 32, 44, 60, 61, 63
Saint Lawrence River ix, 78, 111, 170
Saint Lawrence Valley 132, 167, 168
Saint Mary's Lake 114
Saint Mary's Valley 115
Salinas River 47
Salmon River 16
salt 126, 132, 163
Salt Lake City (Utah) 37, 162
Salton Sea 2, 45, 48
San Andreas Fault (California) vii, 1–2, 6, 37, 41, 45, 47, 48, 177–178
San Bernardino (California) 48
San Bernardino Mountains 45, 49
sand 95, 97, 103, 104, 106, 112, 127, 130, 136, 138, 140, 143, 152, 168
sandbar 139
San Diego (California) 2, 48
sand plain *see* outwash plain
sand spit 99
sandstone 187*t*
  in Adirondacks 167
  in Appalachians 60, 63
  in Black Hills 169
  in Catskills 126, 127
  at Cedar Breaks National Monument 51
  cementing of 79
  on Colorado Plateau 50
  composition of 147
  Connecticut Valley loss of 100
  in Cumberland Mountains 55

dinosaur tracks in 162
fossils in 159, 160
Holyoke Range loss of 68
identification of 153
across New York State 129
at Niagara Falls 128
in Ozarks 84
at Pinnacle Rocks State Park 133
quartzite converted from 150, 168
Redoubt Number Ten loss of 138
in Sugarloaf Mountains 69
Tuscaloosa sandstone 140
in Watchung Mountains 61
at Watkins Glen *125*
weathering of 72–73, 152
San Francisco (California) vii, 1–2, 90, 178
San Francisco Bay 1, 47
San Jose (California) 1
San Pablo Bay 47
Santa Barbara (California) 48
Santa Clara (California) 1
Santa Clara Valley 47
Santa Cruz (California) 1, 47
Santa Cruz Mountains 1
Saratoga Springs (New York) 168
scablands 15
Scandinavia 175, 183*t*
schist 92, *148,* 149–150, 152, 153, 167, 168, 187*t*
Schoharie Creek 123
Scioto River 112–113
scoria 18
"scratches" 95
seashells *82, 134,* 137, 139, 158, 163
sea stacks 24, 47
Seattle (Washington) viii, 6, 7, 22, 25, 27, 28, 117
seaweed *158*
sediment
    Anchorage built on 3
    on Appalachian Plateau 133
    in Appalachians 62
    in Catskill Delta 130
    on Catskills Plateau 126
    on Coastal Plain **137–141**
    from Devonian Period 34
    glaciers and 101, 106
    in Grand Canyon 49
    on Great Plains 81, 121
    on Gulf Coastal Plain 140

in Mississippi River 127
in New York State 78, 127
in Ouchita Mountains 79
Permian sediments 82
in Rocky Mountains 120
settling out of 119
stratification of 108
on Texas coastal plain vi
vegetation sustained by 168
sedimentary rock 186*t,* 187*t*
    age of 156
    Colorado Plateau loss of 50
    formation of 143
    fossils in 157–160
    identification of 152–153
    in Letchworth State Park 127
    types of **147**
    up-ended strata *71*
    weathering of 150
Seldovia (Alaska) 5
Seneca Lake *126,* 132
Sequoia National Park 39, 45
Seward (Alaska) 5
shale 187*t*
    in Boston area 66–67
    composition of 147
    Connecticut Valley loss of 100
    crystallization of 148–149
    on Cumberland Plateau 134
    in early Adirondacks 168
    in early Appalachians 60
    fossils in 159, 160, 165
    Holyoke Range loss of 68
    identification of 153
    in Letchworth State Park 127
    mud hardened into 79
    across New York State 129
    at Niagara Falls 128
    on Ozark Plateau 84
    in Vermont thrust fault 54
    weathering of 72–73, 152
    in western New England 74
Shasta, Mount vi, 46–47
Shawangunk Mountain 129, *131*
Shenandoah River 74, 77
Shenandoah Valley 77, *134*
"Ship Rock" 52, 93

Shuksan, Mount viii, 21, 116
Sierra Nevada 30–32, 39, 42–44, 46
sills 61
silt 104, 147, 159
Silurian Period 129, 184*t,* 185*t*
Silurian Sea 132
silver vii, 169
sinkholes 136, 140
skiing vii, viii
Skyline Drive (Virginia) 76–78
slate 72, 79, 149, 152, 153, 187*t*
"Sleeping Giant" (New Haven, Conn.) 60, 100, 101
sloths 48
Smoky Mountains 134
Snake River 15, *16,* 41, 180
snakes 30
Snoqualamie Pass 115
snow 28, 29, 31, 42
solar system 183*t*
Solduc Hot Springs 23
South America vi, 11–12, 161, 175
South Atlantic Ocean 175
South Dakota viii, 167
Southern Pine Hills 140
Southern Plains 140
Southington (Connecticut) 100, 101
South Meriden (Connecticut) 101
South Peabody (Massachusetts) 93
South Wellfleet (Massachusetts) 99, 100
specific gravity 154–155
spheroidal weathering 152
Spirit Lake 7, 9
spirits v
Spokane (Washington) 30, 115
Springer Mountain 133
spruce trees 28–29, 64, 91, 133
Spy Pond 102
Staten Island (New York City borough) 98
Steven Pass 115
stone fences 93
Stone Mountain 64, *66,* 152
stratification lines 104, 108, 109, 152, 153
stream piracy 74
striations 90, 94, 95, 99
strip mines 164
Stroudsburg (Pennsylvania) 98
subduction zones 177
subsidence 82
Sudbury (Massachusetts) 103
Sugarloaf Mountains 69

Sunset Cliffs (California) 48
Sunset Crater 49
Superior, Lake viii, ix, 34, 167, 169
superposition 49, 156
Susquehanna River 110, 137–138
swamps 35, 98–99, 139
syenite 186*t*
synclines 84
Syracuse (New York) 110

T

Tacoma (Washington) viii, 22, 116
Taconic Mountains 59, 78, 79, 132
talc 155
tapirs 48
Teays River 112
Tennessee 133, 135
Tennessee River 122, 136
Ten Thousand Smokes, Valley of 11
terminal moraines 90, **96–99,** 112–113
terraces 139
terranes 161, 177–180, **177–180**
Tertiary Period 184*t,* 185*t*
Teton Mountain Range 38
Texas 79, 80, 81, 159
Thielson (Washington) 18
Three Fingered Jack 18
Three Sisters 18
thrust faults 37, 54, 56, 66, *67,* 74, 78, 133
thunderstorms 28
Tibetan Plateau 31
tigers *see* saber-toothed tigers
tills 110
Timberline Lodge (Oregon) viii
Timpanogos Cave National Monument 50
Toby, Mount 69–70
Tom, Mount 60, 68
topaz 155
tourism viii, ix, 171
Tower of the Virgin 51
trachyte 186*t*
Trans-Canada Highway ix, 96, 170, 171
transverse fault 37, 46–47
    See also fault lines
trap ridges 60, 61, 76, 101
trap rock 100
tree ferns 164
tree fossils 15, 34, 123, *124,* 164, 165
Triassic Period 33, 70, 162, 184*t,* 185*t*
Trinity River 140
Tristan da Cunha 174
tsunami 5–6
Turnagain Inlet (Alaska) 87

Tuscaloosa sandstone 140
Tuscarora Mountains 73
Tyrannosaurus 162

U

Uinta Mountains 38
Union Peak 18
upended strata 74, 134
uranium 156–157, 170
Utah
    Clorado Plateau 38
    dinosaur remains vi
    Great Salt Lake 41
    lava fields 12, 19
    Uinta Mountains 38
    Wasatch Mountain
        Range 37
Utes 52
Utica (New York) 109

V

Valdez (Alaska) 5
Valley Head Moraines 110
valley trains 110
Vancouver (Canada) ix, 6,
    22, 170
Vancouver Island 178
vegetation
    on Cascades 26, 29–30
    on Cumberland Plateau
        135
    decay of 72, 139–140
    along Hurricane Ridge
        23
    on mountains of past
        168
    on Olympic Mountains
        28
    on San Francisco high-
        lands 27
Venezuela 81
Vermillion Range 169
Vermont vii, 79, 168

Vernal (Utah) 162–163
vesicular basalt 18
Vesuvius, Mount 44, 59
Virginia 72, 138, 160 see
    also Blue Ridge Mountains
volcanic glass see obsidian
volcanic neck vii
volcanoes
    in Alaska 10, 59
    in Appalachians 55–57,
        60–63
    in Boston area 56
    in Cascades 10
    composite volcanoes
        63
    eruptions ix, 6–12, 22
    fossils and 166
    in Hawaii 8
    in Iceland 175–176
    igneous rocks and 143
    in Italy 59
    in Mammoth Lakes 42–
        43
    midocean ridges 173–
        177
    mountain building and
        32
    Mount Baker 10
    Mount Hood 10
    Mount Saint Helens ix
    Newberry volcano 17
    Pinnacles National Mon-
        ument 47
    "Ship Rock" myth 52
    Sunset Crater 49
    in the West **7–12**
    in Yellowstone Park 39

W

Walker Mountain 18
Walnut Canyon 49
Wasatch Range 37, 41–42
Washington, Mount 64, 91–
    92, 93, 94

Washington State
    fossils 163
    ginkgo trees 15
    glaciers 88, 89, 116
    lava fields 13
    Mount Baker viii
    Mount Rainier viii, 20–
        21
    Mount Saint Helens ix,
        7–9, 12
    Mount Shuksan viii
    weather patterns 25–26,
        28, 30
Washington Street (Boston,
    Mass.) 67
Watchung Mountains 61
waterfalls 14, 22, 102, 127
water gaps 74, 78
Watertown Lakes National
    Park (Canada) ix
Watkins Glen (New York)
    110, 125, 126, 127, 132
wave-cut terraces 139
Wayland (Massachusetts)
    103
weather **25–32,** 48
wells 80
Westerly (Rhode Island) 98
westerly winds 25
Weston (Massachusetts)
    103
West Rock (New Haven,
    Conn.) 60, 100
West Virginia viii, 54, 122,
    133, 160, 165
White Mountains (Nevada)
    43
White Mountains (New
    Hampshire) vii, 34, 64, 79,
    91, 92
White River 84, 117
White River Glacier 117
Whitney, Mount 20, 42, 179
Whittier (Alaska) 5

Wichita Mountains 35, 80
Willey Brook 91
Willey Mountain 91
wind 25–28, 31
wind gaps 74, 78, 136
Wind River Mountains 178
Winnipeg (Canada) 170
Winslow (Arizona) 49
wireless telegraphy 99
Woods Hole (Massachu-
    setts) 100
Worcester (Massachusetts)
    103
worm holes 34
Wrangell Mountains 179
Wupatki National Monu-
    ment 49
Wyoming vi, 120

Y

Yakima (Oregon) 29
Yale University 162
Yellowstone National Park
    10, 15, 38, 39, 166
Yellowstone River 14, 120
York River 137–138
Yorktown terraces 138
Yosemite Falls 44, 91
Yosemite National Park 39,
    44, 91
Yosemite Valley 44, 45, 90
Yucatan Peninsula 81
yucca plants 48
Yukon Territory 171, 180

Z

Zion National Park 50–51